Home Office Research Study 293

A gap or a chasm?
Attrition in reported rape cases

Liz Kelly, Jo Lovett and Linda Regan
Child and Woman Abuse Studies Unit,
London Metropolitan University

The views expressed in this report are those of the authors, not necessarily those of the Home Office (nor do they reflect Government policy).

Home Office Research, Development and Statistics Directorate
February 2005

Home Office Research Studies

The Home Office Research Studies are reports on research undertaken by or on behalf of the Home Office. They cover the range of subjects for which the Home Secretary has responsibility. Other publications produced by the Research, Development and Statistics Directorate include Findings, Statistical Bulletins and Statistical Papers.

The Research, Development and Statistics Directorate

RDS is part of the Home Office. The Home Office's purpose is to build a safe, just and tolerant society in which the rights and responsibilities of individuals, families and communities are properly balanced and the protection and security of the public are maintained.

RDS is also part of National Statistics (NS). One of the aims of NS is to inform Parliament and the citizen about the state of the nation and provide a window on the work and performance of government, allowing the impact of government policies and actions to be assessed.

Therefore –

Research Development and Statistics Directorate exists to improve policy making, decision taking and practice in support of the Home Office purpose and aims, to provide the public and Parliament with information necessary for informed debate and to publish information for future use.

First published 2005
Application for reproduction should be made to the Communications and Development Unit, Room 201, Home Office, 50 Queen Anne's Gate, London SW1H 9AT.
© Crown copyright 2005   ISBN 1 84473 555 9
                           ISSN 0072 6435

In 1998 the Home Office announced the Crime Reduction Programme (CRP), which aimed to develop and implement an integrated approach to reducing crime and making communities safer. As part of this programme the Violence Against Women Initiative (VAWI), was launched in July 2000, and specifically aimed to find out which approaches and practices were effective in supporting victims and tackling domestic violence, rape and sexual assault. Thirty-four multi-agency victim focused projects were funded and aimed to develop and implement a range of interventions for various population groups in a number of different settings and contexts. The projects were originally funded until the end of March 2002; however, 24 of these projects had their funding, and in some cases, their evaluations extended until the end of March 2003. A further 24 'Second Round' projects were funded in March 2001; however, these were provided with specific service provision funding and were not evaluated by the Home Office.

For evaluation purposes, the projects were divided into nine packages and projects with similar solutions or strategies, as well as those operating in the same contexts were grouped together. Seven different independent evaluation teams were commissioned to assess the projects in terms of their development, impact and costs. The findings from all of the evaluations have been collated and a series of research reports and concise practitioner focused guides have been published.

This report presents findings from the evaluation of two Sexual Assault Referral Centres (SARCs), one non-centre based support service and three comparison areas where there was no specialist provision for victims. The report provides a valuable insight into the process of attrition in reported rape cases in the Criminal Justice System (CJS), with a specific focus on early withdrawal by complainants. The report provides recommendations for good practice which will be of interest to a range of professionals who have a role or an interest in reducing attrition in reported rape cases in the CJS.

Crime Reduction Programme: Violence Against Women Initiative other reports in the series

Domestic Violence

Douglas, N., Lilley, S.J., Kooper, L. and Diamond A. (2004) *Safety and justice: sharing personal information in the context of domestic violence- an overview.* Home Office Development and Practice Report No. 30. London: Home Office.

Hester, M. and Westmarland, N. (2005) *Tackling Domestic Violence: effective interventions and approaches.* Home Office Research Study No. 290. London: Home Office.

Mullender, A. (2004) *Tackling Domestic Violence: providing support for children who have witnessed domestic violence.* Home Office Development and Practice Report No. 33. London: Home Office.

Parmar, A., Sampson, A. and Diamond, A. (2005) *Tackling Domestic Violence: providing advocacy and support to survivors of domestic violence.* Home Office Development and Practice Report. No. 34. London: Home Office.

Parmar, A., Sampson, A. and Diamond, A. (2005) *Tackling Domestic Violence: providing advocacy and support to survivors of domestic violence from Black and other minority ethnic communites.* Home Office Development and Practice Report. No. 35. London: Home Office.

Taket, A., Beringer, A., Irvine, A. and Garfield, S. (2004) *Tackling Domestic Violence: exploring the health service contribution.* Home Office Online report 52/04. London: Home Office. [Available online at: http://www.homeoffice.gov.uk/rds/onlinepubs1.html]

Taket, A. (2004) *Tackling Domestic Violence: the role of health professionals.* Home Office Development and Practice Report No. 32. London: Home Office.

Rape and sexual assault

Lovett, J., Regan, L. and Kelly, L. (2004) *Sexual Assault Referral Centres: developing good practice and maximising potentials.* Home Office Research Study No 285. London: Home Office.

Regan, L., Lovett, J. and Kelly, L. (2004) *Forensic nursing: an option for improving responses to reported rape and sexual assault.* Home Office Online Report 28/04. [Available online at: http://www.homeoffice.gov.uk/rds/onlinepubs1.html]

Regan, L., Lovett, J. and Kelly, L. (2004) *Forensic nursing: an option for improving responses to reported rape and sexual assault.* Home Office Development and Practice Report No. 31. London: Home Office.

Skinner, T. and Taylor, H. (2005) *Providing counselling, support and information to survivors of rape: an evaluation of the Surviving Rape and Trauma After Rape (STAR) young person's project.* Home Office Online Report 51/04.
[Available online at: http://www.homeoffice.gov.uk/rds/onlinepubs1.html]

Acknowledgements

We would like to express our thanks to the many people whose co-operation and assistance was essential to conducting this evaluation. Firstly, to the Crime Reduction Programme: Violence Against Women Initiative, and particularly Alana Diamond for her input and support throughout. Secondly, to the staff at St Mary's, REACH and STAR, police officers in the Greater Manchester, Northumbria, West Yorkshire, Metropolitan (Brent and Newham) and Thames Valley force areas, and the many individuals in associated agencies, whose commitment was critical to the success of this project. Contributions in terms of data collection and preparation were also made by Dr Tina Skinner, Dr Rosemary Barbaret, Helen Taylor, Val Balding and Carolanne Lyme.

Finally, our sincere gratitude to all the research participants who chose to share their experiences with us. Without them our understanding and this report would have been much the poorer.

Contents

Tables and Figures

Executive summary

Introduction

- Home Office figures show an ongoing decline in the conviction rate for reported rape cases, putting it at an all-time low of 5.6 per cent in 2002. This year-on-year increase in attrition represents a justice gap that the government has pledged to address.
- Rape is a unique crime, representing both a physical and psychological violation. More than with any other crime the victim can experience reporting rape as a form of revictimisation.
- In no other crime is the victim subject to so much scrutiny at trial, where the most likely defence is that the victim consented to the crime. Powerful stereotypes function to limit the definition of what counts as 'real rape'.
- This report draws on material from two evaluation projects funded by the Crime Reduction Programme Violence Against Women Initiative (CRP VAWI). It combines analysis of St Mary's Sexual Assault Referral Centre historic database and prospective case tracking of reported rape/sexual assault cases across six sites over 17-27 months.

Aims and methodology

- The primary aim of the study was to increase understanding of attrition, with an emphasis on early withdrawal from the criminal justice system (CJS) process by complainants.
- Data were collected from three Sexual Assault Referral Centres (SARCs) and three Comparison areas selected to reflect a combination of metropolitan, inner city and rural areas.
- A multi-methodological strategy was employed linking quantitative and qualitative data. The base sample is 3,527 cases, which were tracked prospectively through the CJS. Sub-samples of victims/survivors opted into a series of questionnaires and in-depth interviews (a total of 228 participated). Within this group, police statements and forensic reports were also accessed, where possible. These data were supplemented by expert interviews with key informants and police officers (n=143).

- Whilst this represents the largest data-set in the UK literature on rape and sexual assault, there are some limitations to the study. It proved extremely difficult to recruit research participants in the Comparison areas, so more is known about complainants in areas where there is a SARC. Obtaining information on case outcomes was also problematic in all areas, and there is only final outcome data for two-thirds of the sample.

What we know about rape and attrition

- Findings from the 2001 British Crime Survey (BCS) interpersonal violence module result in a prevalence rate of 0.3 per cent for rape of women over 16 in the year prior to interviews conducted in 2001, and this equates to an estimated annual incidence rate of 47,000 adult female victims of rape. Since the age of 16, 7 per cent of women had suffered a serious sexual assault at least once in their lifetime (5% had been raped). The same study confirms that women are most likely to be raped by men they know, and a considerable proportion reported repeat incidents by the same perpetrator.
- These findings are lower than a previous BCS-based report, and much lower than the prevalence rate in a dedicated study on rape from the early 1990s.
- Analysis of the St Mary's database (covering the years 1987-2002) revealed increasing numbers of young victims aged under 20, and supports the BCS finding that assaults are most likely to be committed by known men.
- Home Office data on reported rape cases in England and Wales show a continuing and unbroken increase in reporting to the police over the past two decades, but a relatively static number of convictions, thus the increasing justice gap.
- Prosecuted cases involving children were more likely to result in conviction than those involving adults.
- All UK studies of attrition in rape cases concur that the highest proportion of cases is lost at the earliest stages, with between half and two-thirds dropping out at the investigative stage, and withdrawal by complainants one of the most important elements.
- A number of studies have found high rates of 'no criming', not limited to the official guidelines for this category.
- Research to date has identified four key points at which attrition occurs: the decision to report; the investigative stage; discontinuance by prosecutors; and the trial. Victim withdrawals can occur at each stage but the highest proportion is evident at the first two points.

Understanding attrition

- Analysis of the data for this study revealed that around one-quarter of reported cases were 'no crimed'; in a proportion of detected cases no proceedings were brought. There was inconsistency in the police classification of case outcomes, particularly among those that were 'no crimed'. The vast majority of cases did not proceed beyond the investigative stage, and the conviction rate for all reported cases was eight per cent.

- Three-quarters of the overall sample reported to the police. Although this was more likely among younger complainants, high reporting levels were also evident among those with disabilities and those involved in prostitution. Cases involving known perpetrators were least likely to be reported. The majority of reports to the police were made within 24 hours.

- Nine per cent of reported cases were designated false, with a high proportion of these involving 16- to 25-year-olds. However, closer analysis of this category applying Home Office counting rules reduces this to three per cent. Even the higher figure is considerably lower than the extent of false reporting estimated by police officers interviewed in this study.

- Evidential issues accounted for over one-third of cases lost at the investigative stage. This group includes cases where: the complainant had learning difficulties, mental health issues or was otherwise unable to give a clear account; DNA testing was not conducted; and an offender was identified but not traced. In a substantial number of cases in this category the decision not to proceed was linked to victim credibility. Consultation between police and Crown Prosecution Service (CPS) rarely led to enhanced case-building.

- Victims who declined to complete the initial investigative process and victim withdrawals accounted for over one-third of cases lost at the police stage. The former was more common in areas where there was no SARC, while the age group most associated with the latter was 16- to 25-year-olds. Key factors in not completing the initial process were being disbelieved and fear of the CJS. Police officers and SARC service user participants also suggested that fear of court was linked to withdrawal.

- Only a small proportion of reported cases were discontinued by the CPS, but this does not accurately reflect their involvement in decision-making, since they were consulted through advice files on many more cases at an earlier point.

- Only 14 per cent of cases reached the trial stage, with a proportion of these not proceeding due to late withdrawal or discontinuance at court. Around half of all convictions were the result of guilty pleas, and where a full trial took place, an acquittal was the more likely outcome. Rates of acquittal were twice as high in cases involving adults as those involving under-16s.

Challenges and dilemmas

- There is an over-estimation of the scale of false allegations by both police officers and prosecutors which feeds into a culture of scepticism, leading to poor communication and loss of confidence between complainants and the police.
- Police officers' early assessments of the difficulties of prosecution and conviction may be interpreted by complainants as discouragement to continue, and fear of the court process can also act as a disincentive.
- There is some evidence of poor investigation and understanding of the law, and in some cases, there has been an emphasis on discrediting features only, by the police and CPS.
- Categorisation of cases by the police is internally inconsistent within and between force areas.
- Alcohol consumption was implicated in a far larger number of cases than drugs. How this contributes to attrition deserves more detailed study.
- Data from service user questionnaires and interviews showed that there are specific elements that would improve responses to reported rape. These include: the availability of female practitioners; a culture of belief, support and respect; access to clear information at appropriate points in the process; being kept informed about case progress; and courtroom advocacy that does justice to the complainant's account.
- From the perspective of complainants, the difference in perceptions between themselves and CJS personnel was too often not just a gap but a chasm. If, however, each point in the attrition process is examined in detail, what emerges is a series of smaller gaps, each of which could be bridged by targeted interventions.

Recommendations

- The most important recommendation from this study is that a shift occurs within the CJS from a focus on the discreditability of complainants to enhanced evidence-gathering and case-building.
- The possibility of inter-agency work between police and specialist support agencies should be further explored with respect to providing support during statement taking and providing information on case status.
- Home Office counting rules for rape and sexual offences need to be revisited in light of the findings from this research: whether cases where there is no evidence

of assault should remain classified as assaults needs to be addressed, and mechanisms should be developed to correct inconsistent classification.

- Guidance should be issued within the police about the timing and content of providing complainants with information about the legal process and the likelihood of a conviction. At a number of points, from the earliest contact on, victims/witnesses perceived this as discouragement from proceeding with the case.

- Development in all areas, through SARCs and/or rape crisis centres, of proactive follow-up of all complainants reporting rape to the police. Such services would add the most value if they combined practical support, advocacy and case-tracking.

- Piloting of early case conferences between police, CPS and counsel, to explore potential evidential weaknesses, and whether these might be addressed through additional evidence, expert testimony, research findings or courtroom advocacy.

- An accredited training course for prosecution barristers, and the development of some form of sanction where briefs are returned or counsel changed just before trial.

- Mechanisms within CPS to monitor courtroom prosecution advocacy, and learn lessons from convictions, acquittals and especially guilty pleas.

- Increased recognition of the significance of alcohol in rape and sexual assault, including further exploration of the extent to which men target unknown women who are drinking and the strategies they use to make initial contact.

- In light of the Sex Offences Act 2003, development of a public education campaign on the meaning of consent and the realities of rape, alongside more detailed training for CJS personnel, explicitly designed to expand the concept of 'real rape'.

1.   Introduction

The most recent Home Office figures on reported rape cases show an ongoing decline in the conviction rate for England and Wales, putting it at an all time low of 5.6 per cent (see Appendix 1). The government has expressed its concern at the year-on-year increase in attrition of reported rape cases, and pledged to address this 'justice gap' not just in relation to rape, but to all reported crime (Home Office, 2002a). There are, however, a number of ways in which rape presents a set of unique challenges. Rape is not just a physical assault but also a violation of personal, intimate and psychological boundaries. Most commonly the offender is known, which also involves a betrayal of trust. It carries particular meanings and potential consequences, which have specific resonances among many of the diverse communities within the UK. More than with any other crime, complainants experience reporting of the rape and the legal process as a form of re-victimisation (Gregory and Lees, 1999; Jordan, 2001a; Temkin, 1997). The reasons for this are historical, with what have been termed 'rape myths' serving to justify:

> *unique case treatment evidenced in corroboration requirements, consent and resistance standards, and the admissibility of victim character evidence.*
> (Caringella-MacDonald, 1985, p66)

Although in most jurisdictions corroboration requirements have been removed from statute, it remains the case that in no other crime is the credibility of the victim/witness so subject to scrutiny (Archambault and Lindsay, 2001). Rape is also unique in that the most likely and also successful defence is to claim that the victim consented to the crime. Commenting on the legacies of rape laws, two US scholars note:

> *This concern with protecting men from false accusations of rape went beyond the 'not guilty until proven innocent' standard, and led to arguments of nearly unlimited admissibility of evidence regarding [the complainant's] character. This combined with cultural conceptions of rape and early rape laws, placed serious impediments on the adjudication of rape cases.*   (Bachman and Paternoster, 1993, p558)

Unlike other crimes, where the status of victim usually confers a sense of deserving sympathy and support, declaring that one has been raped frequently invites judgement, and exacts social and material costs.[1]

---

1. These may include loss of earnings and even giving up a job, and, where the rape took place in the woman's home, a need to move house.

The 'cultural conceptions' of rape referred to here are often described as 'myths', since they do not reflect the reality of rape. We prefer to discuss powerful stereotypes that function to limit the definition of what counts as 'real rape', in terms of the contexts and relationships within which sex without consent takes place. As a number of researchers and legal scholars have pointed out (see, for example, Estrich, 1987; Myhill and Allen, 2002; Du Mont. et al, 2000), despite extensive legal reform, 'real rapes' continue to be understood as those committed by strangers, involving weapons and documented injury. The failure of criminal justice systems to address these stereotypes means that the processes involved in responding to reported rapes – from early investigation through to courtroom advocacy – can serve to reinforce, rather than challenge, narrow understandings of the crime of rape, who it happens to and who perpetrates it. The attrition process itself reflects, and reproduces, these patterns.

> Attrition presents problems other than low conviction rates. It both originates in and leads to the perpetuation of myths and differential treatment of rape cases as compared to all other crimes. (Caringella-MacDonald, 1985, p66)

The comment made in March 2002 by Crown Court Recorder Jonathan Davies (*Daily Telegraph*, 12th March), that women[2] are being encouraged to make complaints of 'date rape' that have little chance of conviction, poses the question of whether we face not so much a 'justice gap'[3] but a chasm between the experiences and expectations of complainants and how the justice system actually responds.

Structure of report

In the next chapter an outline is given of the aims of the research, the methodology and data upon which this report is based. Chapter 3 then presents a brief overview of the current knowledge-base on rape and attrition, with reference to UK and international research. In this chapter, the authors also present new data exploring trends and patterns over time, drawing on the St Mary's Sexual Assault Referral Centre database. Chapter 4 examines the research findings on rape and attrition, the authors present selected findings that offer the most purchase on expanding understanding of the processes involved. Chapter 5 concludes with reflections on the challenges and dilemmas arising from the findings and makes a short series of recommendations.

---

2. Throughout this report the authors refer to complainants as women, since the vast majority of those reporting rape are female. Although, where relevant they report any different patterns for male victims/survivors.
3. Defined specifically as 'the difference between the number of crimes which are recorded and the number which result in their perpetrator being brought to justice' (Home Office, 2002a).

2.   Aims and methodology

This research report draws on the evaluation of two projects funded by the Crime Reduction Programme (CRP) Violence Against Women Initiative: Understanding Attrition, Decreasing Early Withdrawals and Developing Best Practice in Response to Reported Rape: St Mary's Centre; and the linked national evaluation of Sexual Assault Referral Centres – SARCs (see Lovett *et al.*, 2004). It combines crime analysis of the St Mary's database with prospective case-tracking across six sites over a period of 17 to 27 months.[4] The aim is to increase our understanding of attrition in reported rape cases, with an emphasis on early withdrawal by complainants, since withdrawal at later stages have been addressed in recent research (Harris and Grace, 1999).

SARCs were established as a way of combining the needs of victims/survivors in the aftermath of rape and criminal justice requirements with respect to the collection of forensic evidence. All three SARCs involved in this study were the 'pioneer' groups established in the late 1980s and early 1990s – St Mary's in Manchester, REACH in Northumbria and STAR in West Yorkshire – and all three also accept self referrals as well as police referrals. The first two are centre-based and operate according to what the authors have called an 'integrated' model, offering: forensic medical examinations; screening for sexually transmitted infections and HIV counselling; prescription of post-coital contraception and pregnancy testing; telephone information and support; and one-to-one counselling. STAR is not centre-based, it offers support and counselling across the West Yorkshire region through a large group of volunteers and sessional counsellors. Here forensic examinations are 'outsourced' to a third party, which co-ordinates a group of forensic doctors and uses a number of rape examination suites (for more details see Lovett *et al.*, 2004). The combination of self and police referrals to SARCs offers an insight into the reasons for non-reporting, as well as a non-police route for undertaking research on the process of reporting, investigation and prosecution of rape cases.

Three Comparison areas where no SARC exists were also recruited in the south east of England, where data collection took place through the police (see Appendix 2 for a comparative profile of all six areas participating in this study). These sites were selected to create a sample that would include a combination of metropolitan, inner city and rural

---

4. Negotiating on protocols for data collection at the six sites took varying times to finalise, meaning that data gathering began at different points in time: St Mary's from 1st October 2000 to 31st December 2002 (27 months); STAR and REACH from 1st January 2001 to 31st December 2002 (24 months); the Comparison areas from 1st August 2001 to 31st December 2002 (17 months).

areas, thus permitting broad comparability with the three SARC sites, although it is impossible to make direct comparisons since no two areas in the UK are identical. In addition, as the three SARCs serve large populations, it would have been difficult to replicate this size for the comparisons without having to engage and negotiate with multiple police force areas.[5] As the authors were dependent on the co-operation of senior police officers, force areas where they had existing contacts were approached.

Initially, two areas within the Metropolitan Police force area, Brent and Newham, were engaged. Both are located in densely populated, urban areas with a mixed ethnic profile and have dedicated teams of officers (Sexual Offences Investigative Techniques Officers) trained in dealing with victims of sexual offences based in local police stations. To ensure greater comparability with the SARC areas a third site, Thames Valley, was also included. The area covers a wide range of urban and rural locations, with a less mixed ethnic profile than the two London sites, and also has specialist officers (chaperones). There are very limited specialist services in all three areas. In Brent and Newham forensic services are performed by a contractor and in Thames Valley by a locally co-ordinated pool of forensic examiners. Forensic examinations in all three areas are conducted in rape examination suites in a range of locations. While officers provide information on Victim Support and counselling services, there is no co-ordinated provision of support for complainants or a direct referral system at any of the three Comparison sites. Moreover, referral to Victim Support is not automatic but only takes place where police officers ask, complainants say they wish to receive contact, and the referral processes are followed through.[6] Police officers have no record of whether any individual complainant accesses any form of support from any external agency, including Victim Support.

Data collection

In order to gain both basic and in-depth information, from the perspectives of individual service users as well as the range of agencies involved, seven strands of data collection were undertaken.

- Analysis of the historic data in the St Mary's Centre database.

---

5. Two of the Comparison sites are in the area covered by 'Project Sapphire', the Metropolitan Police's strategic response to reported rape. However, this was launched in January 2001, and only began serious case-tracking at the end of 2003, a while after the evaluation had been conceived and the methodology designed.

6. This is in line with current Home Office recommended practice (see Home Office Circular 44/2001, www.homeoffice.gov.uk/docs/hoc44.html).

- Prospective case-tracking[7] using a specially designed database which records demographic data, basic details of the case, reporting of the incident, whether a forensic medical was performed, progress of the legal case and take-up of services.
- Pro formas sent to investigating police officers.[8]
- Questionnaires to service users in the first, fifth and twelfth months after initial contact/report. Options of completing the questionnaire by hand, doing a telephone interview and/or doing a face-to-face interview were offered.
- Interviews with SARC staff, police officers and other key informants (Crown Prosecution Service (CPS), Victim/Witness Support, Forensic Examiners).[9]
- An audit of a sample of forensic medical reports.
- Content analysis of a sample of victim/witness statements.

The total data corpus is presented in Table 2.1 and a full description of the research tools and data sources can be found in Appendix 3.

St Mary's has the most extensive database on recent rapes in the UK, comprising almost 6,500 cases over 13 years prior to the start of the research, and 7,931 by the end of the project. This rich resource had never been analysed, and combined with the authors' case-tracking database it forms the basis of analysis which explores whether there are changing patterns with respect to: the profile of victims and perpetrators; the relationship between victims and offenders; the contexts in which the assaults occur; decision-making regarding reporting; repeat victimisation and offending; and possible correlations with variables such as gender, age, employment status and ethnicity. Several of these have been proposed as factors accounting for the decline in convictions, making the analysis directly relevant to the study of attrition.

The prospective case-tracking across all six sites means that through triangulation with service user questionnaires and interviews, and police pro formas, it has been possible to explore the decision-making processes of complainants and the factors associated with early withdrawals. All data relating to service users were linked using unique reference numbers, enabling cross-referencing across the entire range of data sources.

---

7. The prospective element of the study involved tracking progress through the Criminal Justice System of all reported rape and serious sexual assault cases in the six areas. Most previous UK research on reported rape has used a retrospective design, drawing samples from police and/or CPS case files.
8. This was used in all sites except STAR, where a dedicated case-tracker compiles case outcomes on the project database. Anonymised data from this resource were uploaded into the case-tracking database at six-monthly intervals.
9. Where these are quoted in the text the date of the interview is also included.

Table 2.1: Total and projected data collection 1st October 2000 – 31st December 2002

Data source	St Mary's	REACH	STAR[1]	Comparison	Total	Original projected total
Case tracking data						
Prospective case-tracking data:	1,442	638	1,092	355	3,527	2,000
● client details sheets	1,442	638	1,092	355	3,527	
● initial police pro forma	889	337	836	349	2,411	
● follow-up police pro forma	686	271	836	291	2,084	
Service user questionnaires:						
● questionnaire 1	66	51	91	20	228	250
● questionnaire 2	23	32	59	11	125	130
● questionnaire 3	20	22	36	7	85	100
Interviews with service users	12	17	20	7	56	80
Interviews with staff and key informants	48[2]	20[3]	42[4]	26[5]	136[6]	43
Police statements[7]	31	0	19	n/a	50	100
Forensic medical reports	100	9	0	n/a	109	130

Notes
1 All STAR cases reported to the police, data downloaded from STAR project database.
2 34 individuals.
3 20 individuals, REACH staff interviewed by Rosemary Barberet and police officers by Helen Taylor.
4 39 individuals interviewed by Tina Skinner and Helen Taylor.
5 26 individuals.
6 120 individuals.
7 See Appendix 3 for reasons for low response.

Data analysis

Analysis of the prospective case-tracking data consisted primarily of basic frequency counts and cross-tabulations using the Access database package. Questionnaire data were entered onto SPSS for Windows and, where appropriate, statistical significance tests (Chi-square) were conducted. In addition, all responses to open-ended questions were typed into text files related to each question. These were then grouped thematically and coded for frequency of responses. Interview data were analysed using a similar process of 'consolidation' – collecting all responses to particular questions in a single text file, undertaking coding and content analysis to reveal areas of similarity and difference. Where appropriate, the authors report on numbers and percentages of interview respondents who expressed particular views and opinions.

Not only is this study based on a much more extensive body of data than previous attrition studies (see Table 3.44), cases have been tracked prospectively, rather than retrospectively. In addition, the unique case numbers mean that whilst the entire data-set is anonymised, all data sources, apart from the interviews with professionals, can be examined by case. The importance of this was graphically illustrated when analysis of the police pro formas was undertaken to examine the reasons for cases dropping out at the early stages. The explanations provided by police officers created a sense of many deeply problematic cases; it was only when these were compared with the perceptions of the complainants in these same cases that a possible alternative narrative emerged.

Defining terms

Attrition is the process by which rape cases drop out of the legal process, thus do not result in a criminal conviction. Some would argue that the first, and in many ways most significant, point of attrition is the failure to report the crime (see more detailed discussion in Chapter 3). As the three SARCs involved in this study support a proportion of service users who have not reported to the police, the authors have been able to present some findings on unreported cases (see Chapter 4, Attrition point 1). However, since both public concern and government pronouncements about the 'justice gap' have been articulated in terms of the falling proportion of convictions in relation to increasing numbers of recorded rape cases, subsequent findings (see Chapter 4, Attrition points 2-7) and overall analysis of the attrition process (see Tables 4.1 and 4.2) are based only on reported cases.

In previous studies of attrition, two alternate conventions have been employed in the presentation of conviction rates (cases resulting in a finding or plea of guilt): as a proportion of all prosecuted cases or the proportion of all reported cases. In this study the conviction rate is defined according to the latter convention, although a figure for the former is also presented.

In terms of the sample, when referring to service user participants the term 'respondents' is used for those completing questionnaires and 'interviewees' for the sub-sample who also undertook in-depth interviews.

Limitations

Table 2.1 summarises the data corpus, comparing the actual data collected with that projected in the bid to the CRP. In some areas the anticipated numbers were exceeded, such as: the number of cases in the case-tracking database; and the interviews with staff and key informants. In other cases the targets were not reached, especially with respect to the involvement of service users through questionnaires and interviews. Below the key issues that affected the different areas of data collection are outlined.

At the design stage of this project the intention was to use the St Mary's historic database to explore changes over time with respect to the declining conviction rate. The database is a unique resource in the UK containing cases since the project was founded in 1986 (when the conviction rate was 19%). However, it emerged that not only was the database unstable and using 'ancient' software (for which there was no longer any technical support), but data entry was inconsistent and especially poor for the early years. A number of these problems were, eventually, overcome: a new database was designed, data imported, and data checked and inputted for the most problematic years.[10] Whilst the historic database does offer material not previously available, it has limited data on attrition, since case outcomes have not been routinely recorded. The authors' experience with the case-tracking database exposed how time-consuming and frustrating it can be chasing outcome data from a large number of police divisions. It also highlighted a clear gap in local inter-agency responses to rape and sexual assault.[11] Despite these limitations, the database offers insights into the broader contexts of rape based on a substantial data set.

10. This process took years rather than months after the researchers identified the problems early in the research. An offer to provide the already designed prospective case-tracking database was refused by the Health Trust, and a lengthy tendering process with preferred suppliers undertaken. Installation and transfer of data took months, rather than the few weeks anticipated, and data from some key fields was not initially transferred. As a consequence, the researchers, only had access to the historic data a few weeks before the research funding ended.
11. STAR is the only SARC to have a dedicated case-tracker, whose responsibility is to ensure case progress and current status is known and recorded. Even here, however, for the data covering this project we had to classify four per cent (n=32) of STAR cases had to be classified as 'unknown' in terms of the authors' classification system.

Although a higher than anticipated number of cases was recorded on the case-tracking database, considerable time had to be devoted to updating case outcomes (using pro formas to the police at two points in time, within a couple of months of the initial report and approximately a year afterwards, in all areas except STAR, where the data were extracted from their case-tracking database), and getting returns from the Comparison areas. Whilst outcomes have been entered for over two-thirds of the whole sample, it proved impossible to access information on a significant proportion, despite regular requests for missing data. Where data from the police pro formas were used these covered cases from St Mary's, REACH and the Comparison areas. Whilst there are classification and outcome data from STAR, these were downloaded from their database and consist of information recorded by the STAR case-tracker rather than by police officers. Outcome data should be taken as indicative rather than absolute for two reasons, firstly, not all the pro formas were returned (2,643 cases were reported to the police but at the end of the evaluation both police pro formas were missing for 232). Secondly, the amount of detail in the section requesting reasons for decisions varied considerably, both between individual officers and in terms of who had taken the decision (where it was a police decision more information was provided than when it was the complainant's). This is obviously a limitation of the study, highlighting the difficulties of prospective research across multiple sites and where the actions of multiple parties are under scrutiny.

Since the primary focus was on the earliest stages of the process, which has been less researched than the CPS and trial stages (see, for example, Harris and Grace, 1999; HMCPSI, 2002; Lees, 2002), data collection from the police was prioritised. Similar processes were not developed with the CPS, and when towards the end of the project the authors attempted to address the large number of unknowns in that category, it was discovered that the official police numeric identifiers the authors had been using to track cases were not those used by the CPS. The only way these outcomes could have been obtained would have involved compromising the confidentiality agreement made with the SARCs at the outset. Therefore, the data for the final stages were not as detailed, although the ultimate outcomes, where known, are accurate.

The main reason for the lower than projected level of service user/complainant participation is the very low take-up in the Comparison areas, where all layers of data collection proved more problematic for two reasons: the police areas had far less investment in the research, since they were not part of CRP-funded projects; and repeated changes in staff, for example the key contact with the research team frequently changed, and the new person usually received no hand-over information.. Different timings of first contact were experimented, in respect to the research across the three SARCs. One clear lesson was that delaying this until at least a month after attending the SARC (as occurred at REACH and STAR) prompted higher take-up (see Appendix 4 for response rates at all sites).

Other researchers have noted the difficulty of engaging women in research who have recently been raped (see, for example, Harris and Grace, 1999; Jordan, 2001a), citing both a reluctance to discuss the painful issues and difficulties in tracing individuals. Both of these factors were evident in this project, alongside a level of 'gate-keeping', with those who researchers rely on for access seeking to 'protect' victims/survivors from what they fear may be perceived as unnecessary intrusion. As part of their research practice with victims/survivors, the authors always included questions on the meaning and impact of participation. In every project, and this is with no exception, hardly anyone reported negative impacts and many have noted ways in which they found participation useful. Many have commented that they hope their involvement might lead to an improvement in responses by the criminal justice system to other victims (for more details see Lovett et al., 2004).

Despite not achieving the original targets, the participating sample is larger than in any previous UK study of attrition (see Table 3.4 below), and compares favourably to a number of international studies (see Chapter 3). It also broadly reflects the overall socio-demographic profile of the 3,527 service users and complainants from the SARC and Comparison areas registered in the case-tracking database.[12] A total of 228 first questionnaires were returned (66 from St Mary's, 51 from REACH, 91 from STAR and 20 from the Comparison sites). The 228 respondents were mainly female, white and were aged under 35. However, there were 14 male participants, 12 from Black or other minority ethnic backgrounds and the average age was slightly older than the overall case-tracking sample at 30 years. Over half (53%, n=121) of the assaults had been committed by men known to the victims, with just over one-third by recent acquaintances (13%, n=30) or strangers (24%, n=55). The nature of the relationship with the perpetrator was unknown in the remaining ten per cent (n=22) of cases. While the majority were police referrals to the service, over one-third were self-referrals (36%, n=81). All those in the Comparison areas reported directly to the police. In terms of attrition, research participants (questionnaire respondents and interviewees) were more likely than the case-tracking sample as a whole to have cases detected and proceeded with (26%, n=49), and for the case to reach court (23%, n=38).[13] Since this was a prospective study, these outcomes could not have been anticipated at the early point when participants opted into the research. Those who chose to be interviewed were all female (n=56), except two, and were noticeably older, with an average age of 32 years; they were even more likely to have their case proceed to court (37%, n=16 of 43 who reported) and had a higher conviction rate than in the case-tracking sample (21%, n=9). Revealingly, though, most interviewees, including those where the legal outcome was positive, expressed dissatisfaction with elements within the criminal justice process.

12. This is based on analysis using the case-tracking database of all service users in the SARCs areas and complainants in the Comparison areas (n=3,527), compared with the sub-group of those who participated in the research (n=228). For a detailed profile of the overall case-tracking sample see Lovett et al., 2004.
13. In the case-tracking sample 20 per cent (n=527) of reported cases proceeded, while 14 per cent (n=322) reached the court stage.

It could be argued that by drawing the sample from SARCs the majority in this study have better experiences of reporting rape, and therefore the more negative experiences of complainants elsewhere are underestimated. Whilst it is to be hoped that complainants would have better experiences in areas with a SARC than those areas without one, it is overly simplistic to presume this for every case for a number of reasons: there are differences in the services offered by the three SARCs, and there is no control over the location or conduct of forensic examinations (see Lovett *et al.*, 2004); service user data revealed variability of experience both within and between SARCs; police practice may or may not be affected by the presence of a SARC, with police and CPS' decision-making more likely to be the outcome of national policies and widely held perspectives than local variations in service provision for victims.

3.   What we know about rape and attrition

Understanding attrition requires not only close examination of previous research on this topic, but also a basic grounding in the current knowledge on rape – how common it is, the contexts in which it occurs and the proportion of cases that are reported. In this chapter recent research is presented on the incidence and prevalence of rape, as well as findings from the St Mary's historic database identifying patterns and trends over time with respect to the profile of reported rapes. Key UK and international research on attrition is also presented.

How common is rape?

Measurements of the prevalence of rape tend to be of two kinds – those assessing its occurrence over lifetime, and those examining its extent within more limited time periods, such as a year or before the age of 16. The number of reported rapes is lower than both incidence and prevalence rates, since rape remains one of the most under-reported crimes (Walby and Allen, 2004). Official figures for reported assaults often include children, as in many jurisdictions, including England and Wales, there is no separate crime of child rape.[14]

Whilst there have been far fewer studies of the prevalence of sexual assault than of domestic violence (Hagemann-White, 2001; Kelly and Regan, 2001), access to relatively accurate official statistics for reported rapes has been more straightforward. Researching unreported rape and sexual assault has proved more complex than many other forms of violence against women, since using the word 'rape' in questions greatly decreases the reporting of forced sex/sex without consent (Schwartz, 1997). The redesign of questions, for example, in the US National Crime Victimisation Study in 1992 resulted in findings four times higher than previous versions (Greenfield, 1997). As with all prevalence research, inconsistent findings are attributed to methodological differences with respect to: the sample; the number and content of questions asked; the format (questionnaire, telephone or face-to-face interview); and the definition of rape/sexual assault used by the researchers (see Schwartz, 1997, for a more detailed discussion). At the same time, comparative data show such significant variations (Australia, the USA and Sweden recording high prevalence rates per head of population, and South Africa had the highest rates for both prevalence and reporting) that the possibility of differential national levels of sexual violence within different societies needs to be explored.

14. There are a range of specific sexual offences against children in the Sexual Offences Act, which was implemented in May 2004. It remains to be seen, however, whether the CPS continue to use the charge of rape for cases involving under-16s.

Incidence and prevalence in the UK

There has been no dedicated national random sample study of either the incidence or prevalence of rape in the UK, as distinct from wider surveys such as the national British Crime Survey (BCS), which focus on the broader issue of 'crime' but include a section on sexual assault. In fact, there has only been a single study designed solely to provide information on the extent of unreported rape (Painter, 1991). This survey involved 1,007 women in 11 cities and was primarily an attempt to quantify the extent of marital rape. The key findings include:

- one in four women had experienced rape or attempted rape in their lifetime;
- the most common perpetrators were current and ex-partners; and
- the vast majority (91%) told no one at the time.

The BCS is a large national victim-focused survey, which is used by the Home Office to provide estimates of the prevalence and incidence of crime in England and Wales. The 1998 and 2000 BCS both included a computerised self-completion module, which was designed to provide an accurate estimate of the extent and nature of sexual victimisation (Myhill and Allen, 2002). In 2001 the BCS included another computerised self-completion module, which this time captured data on interpersonal violence, which was defined as domestic violence, sexual violence and stalking (Walby and Allen, 2004).

Rather unexpectedly, since the ability of the BCS to detect sexual violence has long been subject to criticism and internal reflection at the Home Office (Myhill and Allen, 2002), the findings from the 2001 specially designed interpersonal violence module are lower for sexual violence than in the earlier overview.[15] The last-year prevalence rates calculated for 'sexual victimisation' – rape and sexual assault of women over 16 – are: 0.9 per cent (2002) and 0.5 per cent (2001) for sexual assault and 0.4 per cent (2002) and 0.3 per cent (2001) for rape. The much higher figure for sexual assault in the earlier data (Myhill and Allen, 2002) might be accounted for by the use of a narrower definition in the later study, linked to the revisions in the Sexual Offences Act (Walby and Allen, 2004).[16] Myhill and Allen (2002) extrapolate that their figures would produce an annual incidence for rape of 61,000 in the year before the survey, whereas the figures for the more recent study means the annual incidence rate falls to 47,000 (Walby and Allen, 2004).

---

15. The authors suggest a range of methodological changes that might account for the differences (Walby and Allen, 2004, p116), and sexual violence still tends to be under-reported in surveys that specify they are about 'crime' (Schwartz, 1997).
16. Only incidents that would be defined in law as rape and the new of 'offence of sexual assault by penetration' are included.

The earlier study (Myhill and Allen, 2002) recorded a 20 per cent reporting rate, with the more recent data showing a lower rate of 15 per cent (Walby and Allen, 2004) among those disclosing rape. Note, the focus in the former was whether the 'last' incident was reported, whereas in the latter it refers to the 'worst' incident.

The BCS estimates cannot be simply mapped onto Home Office recorded crime statistics, firstly because not every crime reported is recorded as a crime at all, or as the same crime the victim perceives to have taken place. Secondly, to make the data comparable, disaggregation in terms of gender and age would need to be undertaken.

The prevalence estimates from both studies are considerably lower than in Painter's study (1991): one in ten (9.7%) and one in six (16.6%) women respectively had been sexually assaulted; and one in 20 (4.9%) and one in 27 (3.7%) respectively had suffered at least one incident of rape since they were 16 (Myhill and Allen, 2002; Walby and Allen, 2004). Whilst there is considerable disparity here between the actual numbers[17], there is convergence about the contexts in which rape takes place: women are most likely to be raped by men they know (intimates, 54%, other known individuals, 29%); and a considerable proportion involve repeat assaults by the same perpetrator (50% in the last 12 months) (Walby and Allen, 2004). The Myhill and Allen (2002) report also reflected findings from other jurisdictions (Bergen, 1995; Easteal, 1998) that rapes by current and ex-partners were the most likely to result in injuries. This profile also accounted for the most common locations, which were the victim's home (55%) followed by offender's home (20%), public place (13%) and elsewhere (13%).[18]

Both sets of BCS data confirm an increasing willingness amongst women to tell someone, but even for those raped in the last five years less than half did so. They also echo findings from research on rape, domestic violence and child sexual abuse, that the most likely person to be told is a friend or family member (Kelly, 2000), and that only a small minority access specialist support organisations like SARCs and rape crisis centres (Walby and Allen, 2004, p94; Myhill and Allen, 2002, p48).

17. Considerable discussion has taken place about the subtle and not so subtle methodological differences which result in lower prevalence findings for sexual violence in general crime surveys compared to dedicated studies of either violence against women or rape (see for example, Schwartz, 1997; Hagemann-White, 2001).
18. Here, the authors rely more on Myhill and Allen (2002), which contains extensive contextual data since it is only concerned with rape and sexual assault.

Incidence and prevalence research internationally

International prevalence research sheds further light on some of these issues since several community-based studies have, through a focus only on violence against women (rather than 'crime'), enabled more disclosure. The most frequently cited research was conducted by Statistics Canada in 1992, which involved a national random sample of 12,300 women and used telephone interviews. Whilst most publicity has been given to the domestic violence findings, considerable data were collected on rape and sexual assault (Johnson and Sacco, 1995). The BCS findings on known men and repeat assaults were echoed, but a far higher prevalence rate was found (over one in three reported a sexual assault) and a lower reporting rate to the police (6% compared to 25% for domestic violence in this study).

The Australian Women's Safety Survey conducted by the Bureau of Statistics in 1996 (Easteal, 1998) involved a random sample 6,300 women aged 18 and over. It produced incidence finding of 1.9 per cent for sexual assault in the previous 12 months. Known men accounted for over two-thirds of assailants (68%), and current/ex-partners and dates comprised more than half of this group (an even higher proportion was found in the most recent US study, Tjaden and Thoennes, 1998). Over half of the assaulted women in the sample (59%) had told a friend, and 15 per cent reported to the police.

In her review of studies of 'date' rape Koss (2000) notes similar and higher findings in smaller samples of college students and naval recruits (see, for example, Fisher et al., 2000). She concludes that the trenchant criticisms of the mid-1990s – that samples were unrepresentative, female college students were uniquely vulnerable to rape, and prevalence findings were wildly inconsistent – have all been 'outgrown' through the accumulation and convergence of findings. Archambault and Lindsay (2001) also note the misconception that non-stranger sexual assault is 'date rape'. Their analysis of reported crimes in San Diego (n=894) revealed only 19 per cent took place in the context of dating relationships.

Summary

- There has been no dedicated national random sample UK study of the incidence or prevalence of rape. However, the national victim-focused BCS has included a self-completion module to capture data on rape and sexual assault in the 1998, 2000 and 2001 surveys, within the broader issue of 'crime'.
- A 1991 UK survey found that one in four women had experienced rape/attempted rape in their lifetime, with current and ex-partners the most common perpetrators, and the vast majority not disclosing the crime at the time.

- Findings from the BCS 2001 revealed the prevalence rate for rape of women over 16 was 0.3 per cent for the year prior to interview, and an estimated 47,000 adult female victims of rape. The prevalence rate since the age of 16 is one in 27 women suffering at least one incident of rape.
- The BCS confirms that women are most likely to be raped by men they know, and that a considerable proportion had experienced repeat incidents by the same perpetrator.
- There are international examples of prevalence studies, which through a specific focus on violence against women have enabled greater disclosure.

New data on patterns and trends

Whilst the limitations of the St Mary's historic database have been noted in Chapter 2, it nonetheless represents a unique resource for tracing trends over time and the contexts in which rapes reported to the police take place. Although the authors cannot present attrition figures per se, they have been able to test some of the explanations floated in UK research for the continuing decline in the proportion of convictions.

A large number of calculations and analyses have been undertaken, including cross-tabulations, not all of which are reported here. The key areas investigated were patterns and changes over time with respect to: overall service use; relationship between assailant and victim; location of assault; timings of assaults, including days and months; use of weapons and injuries; and the relevance of demographic factors including gender, age, employment status and ethnicity. Multiple assailant cases were examined in detail, as were individuals who reported multiple assaults by different perpetrators. Several re-codings were developed to make some of these calculations manageable. The most relevant here is a three-way coding for relationship: well known (current/ex-partners, family members), known (friends and acquaintances) and unknown (total strangers, those known for less than 24 hours[19]).

Numbers and age profile of service users

Table 3.1 shows that the number of cases seen at St Mary's has more than doubled since 1987, with the majority of this increase coming from police referrals.

---

19. Archambault and Lindsay (2001) use a similar category of 'brief encounter' analysing San Diego's police data, noting that from the perspective of victims they do not 'know' these individuals.

Table 3.1: **Referrals to St Mary's 1987-2002**

Attendance Year	Number of referrals	% change from prior year	Cumulative total of referrals	5 year % change
1987	301			
1988	346	15%		
1989	408	18%		
1990	399	-2%		
1991	400	0%		
1992	392	-2%	1,945	
1993	463	18%		
1994	457	-1%		
1995	473	4%		
1996	541	14%		
1997	593	10%	2,527	30%
1998	556	-6%		
1999	621	12%		
2000	631	2%		
2001	695	10%		
2002	642	-8%	3,145	24%

Source: St Mary's historic database

Interestingly self-referrals are only slightly higher in 2002 than 1987, and have thus become a decreasing proportion of cases (see Figure 3.1). This is also reflected in the increase in forensic examinations, both overall (from 186 in 1987 to 488 in 2002) and as a percentage of all cases seen: 62 per cent (n=186 of 301) in 1987, 76 per cent (n=488 of 642) in 2002 (see Figure 3.2).

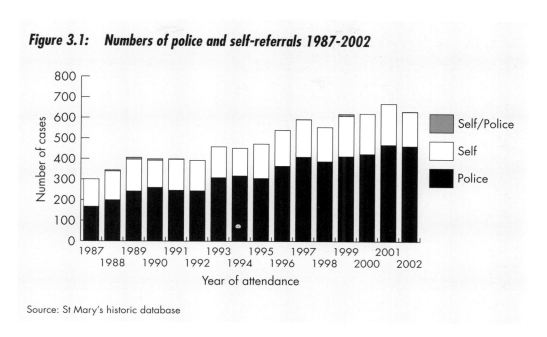

Figure 3.1: Numbers of police and self-referrals 1987-2002

Source: St Mary's historic database

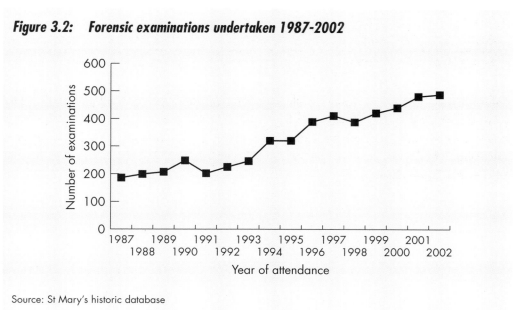

Figure 3.2: Forensic examinations undertaken 1987-2002

Source: St Mary's historic database

A large increase in reports by men is also evident in the St Mary's historic data-set – 280 per cent between 1993-1997 and 87 per cent between 1998-2002 – although they still only account for 8 per cent of all service users.

The age profile of service users has altered slightly, with the proportion of those aged under 20 increasing from 25 per cent in 1988 to a high of 43 per cent of all service users in 2002 (see Figure 3.3). The number of over-45s has remained fairly constant at five per cent. The increase in referrals of under-16s, was the basis of another of the CRP rape projects (see Skinner and Taylor, 2005). A potential age profile has not been explored as a possible element in declining rates of conviction.

Figure 3.3:   Age profile of service users 1987-2002

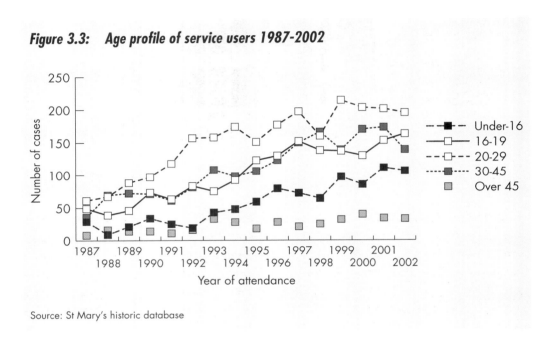

Source: St Mary's historic database

Relationship to offender

Analysis of the relationship between victim and offender for the full data-set (1987-2002) reveals that the largest category of assailants are acquaintances (33%), followed by strangers (28%), current and ex-partners (19%), known less than 24 hours (11%) and family members (10%). Figure 3.4 displays the annual breakdown by relationship type. These figures are closer to the profile found in the BCS data (see earlier section), with the overall proportion of assaults by known men at 57 per cent. Nevertheless, it is clear from both the BCS and this study that stranger assaults are still more likely to be reported to the police/support services, and that assaults by intimates (current and ex-partners) remain under-reported.

Figure 3.4:   *Relationship between victim and perpetrator 1987-2002*

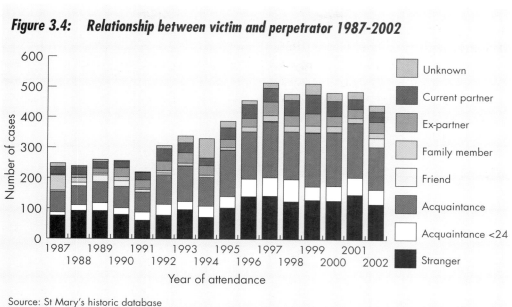

Source: St Mary's historic database

Under 20-year-olds were more likely to report assaults by acquaintances, with assaults by current/ex-partners most common within the 20- to 45-year-old age group. Looking at changes over time (see Figure 3.4), whilst there are shifts they are not of the order or nature that many commentators have suggested: the proportion of stranger assaults has only fallen by six to seven per cent from 1987 to 2002; and the increasing categories are current and former partners, and friends – neither of which can be termed 'date rape'. These data are different from those reported by Harris and Grace (1999), who argue that the fall in the conviction rate throughout the 1990s can be accounted for solely in terms of the different kinds of rape cases being reported. Both the historic data from St Mary's and a recent reassessment of attrition for the same time period as the Harris and Grace study (Lea *et al.*, 2003) do not fully support this contention.

Location of assaults
The most common location in which rape took place was a public place (32%), followed by the victim's home (24%) and perpetrator's home (19%), with vehicles representing six per cent. Again, this profile is different from that in BCS data (see earlier). Almost half (45%) of the assaults reported by women in prostitution took place in vehicles, followed by public places (29%). There was minimal variation over time in the locations of assaults, although more subtle distinctions within public place, which the authors could not track, might reveal some shifts.

Violence and injuries

Whilst research from other jurisdictions suggests that injuries are documented in only a minority of reported rape cases (Kelly, 2003a), they are documented in the majority (an average of two-thirds) of those undergoing a forensic medical at St Mary's. The database also confirms that rapes by well-known perpetrators are slightly more likely to result in injuries (70%). These data suggest there is supportive medical evidence in the majority of cases where forensic medical examinations are conducted in conducive conditions (see Regan *et al.*, 2004).

Time frames

Aggregating cases from 1987-2002 revealed there are two consistent peaks in reporting, during the summer (July and August) for stranger assaults and in the New Year (some of these reports may also relate to the Christmas period) for assaults by known perpetrators (see Figure 3.5).

Figure 3.5: **Reporting of rapes by month of the year and relationship to offender 1987-2002**

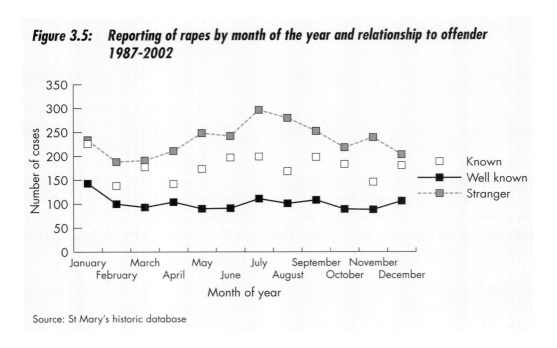

Source: St Mary's historic database

In terms of days of the week, peaks in reporting are Friday to Sunday, although an average of 12 per cent of first attendances at St. Mary's SARC take place on each of the other four weekdays.

Employment status

In terms of the status of service users the largest category is unemployed (27%), followed by students (23%) and those in full-time employment (22%). The high number of students is linked partly to the preponderance of under-20s in the sample overall, and partly to the number of universities and colleges in Greater Manchester. Employment status was correlated with referral type, with a higher proportion of those in full-time work being self, rather than police, referrals. There were also patterns within relationship to offenders, with the full-time employed most likely to be assaulted by unknown assailants (41%), homemakers by assailants known to them (31%) and students by known and unknown assailants (37% and 38% respectively).

Ethnicity

The ethnic profile of attendees has become more diverse, especially in the most recent years, where BME women (there were no BME men in the sample) represent eight per cent of all service users. At first glance it appears that these are most likely to be self-referrals, however, analysis by ethnic group reveals a large group of African asylum seekers seeking support for sexual assaults that took place before they migrated, whilst Pakistani and Black Caribbean women were more likely to be police referrals than other groups, including white women.

Multiple assailants

Eleven per cent of cases involved more than one assailant (n=863), with the majority of these cases involving two (60%) or three (23%), but a significant proportion (17%) four or more – one case involved 14 and another 20 perpetrators. Whilst the number of multiple assailant cases has increased year-on-year, they have not risen as a proportion of cases, in fact they have fallen slightly over the 16-year period. Revealingly, this group is not just made up of strangers either, at least one individual in a third of assaults involving two or three assailants was known to the victim. Current, and, ex-partners, friends and acquaintances featured in multiple assailant cases. In cases involving 10 or more perpetrators (n=7), all the perpetrators were strangers.

Multiple attendees

One issue that has not been addressed in previous studies is the number of service users who report multiple assaults over time. A total of 287 (9%) service users had attended more than once about separate offences. The vast majority (77%, n=221) attended twice, with 44 attending three times, two attending six times and one attending eight times. Possible correlations with either mental health problems or involvement with prostitution were tested, but did not account for these patterns. Whilst the database does not enable further investigation, these data raise the possibility of a group who may be uniquely vulnerable to repeat victimisation. Given the high rates of attrition, and that prior unproven allegations are seen to detract from victim credibility (Jordan, 2004), this group may also, at least for subsequent assaults, have even less access to justice.

Summary

- The number of cases seen at St Mary's has doubled since 1987, with the majority of this increase accounted for by police referrals. The number of forensic examinations conducted has risen proportionately.
- Reported rapes even to a SARC still differ from the profile in prevalence studies.
- The age profile of service users has altered slightly, with under-20s forming a significant and growing proportion of all cases.
- Fifty-seven per cent of assaults were committed by known men, but stranger assaults remain more likely to be reported to the police than those committed by intimates.
- The most common assault locations were public places, followed by victims' and perpetrators' homes.
- In contrast to previous research findings high levels of documented injury were found in the St Mary's sample, and this was more likely in cases where the perpetrator was well known.
- The two peak reporting times are in the summer (July and August) and over the New Year period.
- In terms of employment status, service users were most commonly unemployed, followed by students and full-time employed.
- The ethnic profile of service users has become more diverse.
- Eleven per cent of assaults were perpetrated by more than one assailant.
- Nine per cent of service users reported separate assaults by different perpetrators.

Research on attrition

It is rather surprising, given the extent of statute and procedural reform in many jurisdictions over the last two decades (Schulhofer, 1998; Temkin, 2003), that research on attrition in rape cases is relatively rare. In fact, many European countries cannot even provide basic data on the numbers of reports, prosecutions and convictions (Kelly and Regan, 2001; Regan and Kelly, 2003). In this respect the UK has a stronger track record than many other countries, with a number of published studies and yearly statistics compiled by the Home Office.

UK data and research

Figure 3.6, using official statistics from the Home Office, graphically illustrates the two patterns in reported rape cases in England and Wales over the past two decades: a continuing and unbroken increase in reporting[20]; and a relatively static number of convictions. The combination of these two trends, which began in the 1970s (Regan and Kelly, 2003), means that whilst in 1977 one in three reported rapes resulted in a conviction, by 2002 this had fallen to one in 18 (32% versus 5.6%). The only change to the overall pattern is a small increase in the percentage of prosecutions in 2001, which continues into 2002, but with no parallel increase in convictions. This may be an outcome of changes in local and/or national policy in the police and CPS. However, it is too soon to say whether this will be a sustained trend, which will also feed through into the conviction rate. In fact, the attrition rate is even greater, since official statistics exclude reports that are 'no crimed' very early in the process (see Gregory and Lees, 1999; Harris and Grace, 1999), not to mention that some convictions are overturned on appeal.

Figure 3.6: Attrition in rape cases England and Wales 1985-2002

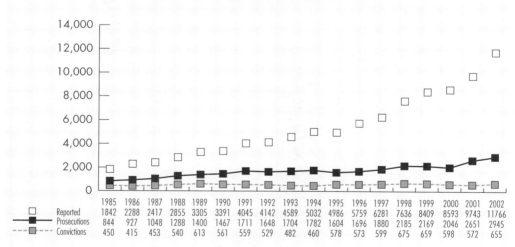

	1985	1986	1987	1988	1989	1990	1991	1992	1993	1994	1995	1996	1997	1998	1999	2000	2001	2002
Reported	1842	2288	2417	2855	3305	3391	4045	4142	4589	5032	4986	5759	6281	7636	8409	8593	9743	11766
Prosecutions	844	927	1048	1288	1400	1467	1711	1648	1704	1782	1604	1696	1880	2185	2169	2046	2651	2945
Convictions	450	415	453	540	613	561	559	529	482	460	578	573	599	675	659	598	572	655

Source: Regan and Kelly, 2003

20. Changes in the National Crime Reporting Standards (NCRS) introduced in April 2002 may have contributed to the increased figures for reported rape, since recording and classification of all crimes should now be based on the perception of the victim that an offence occurred. Simmons and Dodd (2003, p5) suggest that changing this counting rule may have increased recorded offences against the person by 23 per cent in police statistics. "The number of recorded sexual offences was thought to be largely unchanged in 2002/03, after accounting for the effects of the NCRS (reliable estimates for this effect are not available due to the relatively small numbers of occurrences)" (Simmons and Dodd, 2003, p82). This will only have had a marginal effect on the data in this report, however, since the majority cases were reported before this change.

Table 3.2 presents disaggregated data for prosecutions and convictions involving adults and children (under 16-years-olds) for the years 1998-2002, covering all rape and attempted rape cases. Conviction data include guilty pleas; convictions at trial are lower than this overall rate. For adults, around one-quarter of prosecuted cases result in a conviction; the figure was more than one-third for child cases, until a dramatic fall of 12 percentage points from 2000 to 2001, although it recovered very slightly in 2002. Cases considered the 'weakest' evidentially are not referred up to the CPS by the police. These data suggest that even cases deemed relatively strong by police and supported by CPS fare poorly in the later stages of the criminal justice process.

Table 3.2:   **Comparison of prosecution outcomes in adult and child rape cases 1998-2002**

Year	Rapes and attempted rapes adult females and males			Rapes and attempted rapes of of child (under-16) females and males		
	Prosecutions	Convictions	Prosecutions resulting in convictions	Prosecutions	Convictions	Prosecutions resulting in convictions
1998	1366	382	28%	810	291	36%
1999	1319	317	24%	846	335	40%
2000	1245	329	26%	788	264	34%
2001	1528	326	21%	1112	241	22%
2002	1646	352	21%	1288	292	23%

Source: Home Office data

The 2001 and 2002 Home Office data are revealing in other ways (see Appendix 1). Here reporting, prosecution and conviction data are presented by police force area; for the purposes of this report, additional calculations of the conviction rate and rates of reporting by population were undertaken. The conviction rate shows a considerable range between areas, varying from one to 14 per cent across the two years. A number of potential confounding factors were explored, including whether there were higher reporting rates per head of population, but were not linked to the variations in conviction rates in any obvious way.[21] Nor were higher or lower rates simply a function of either metropolitan versus rural areas or the number of cases dealt with per year: areas with conviction rates above ten per cent in 2002 (Cleveland, Cumbria, Gwent, South Wales and South Yorkshire) and those

21. There were, however, interesting variations in the number of notifiable offences per 100,000: taking the 2002 data, the majority of force areas had rates of between 15 and 25 (n=25), nine areas had rates of below 15 and eight rates of more than 25. The higher rates were not associated with Metropolitan areas, apart from London that had the highest overall.

with rates below four per cent (Avon & Somerset, Essex, Gloucestershire, Leicestershire, Sussex, Warwickshire and West Yorkshire) were not distinguishable on these grounds. In addition, variations of plus or minus five per cent were evident for a number of areas between 2001 and 2002 – a considerable increase or fall given the current low average rate of convictions. Additional research, over longer timescales and drawing on more detailed case data, is undoubtedly needed if variations both between and within police force areas are to be understood and accounted for.

Table 3.3 compares five UK research studies (Chambers and Millar, 1983; Grace et al., 1992; Lees and Gregory, 1993; Jamieson et al., 1998[22]; Harris and Grace, 1999; Lea et al., 2003) alongside data from St Mary's Sexual Assault Referral Centre for 1996-1997[23]. Four of the studies comprise data from England and Wales, and two (Chambers and Millar, 1983; Jamieson et al., 1998) focus on Scotland. It has been less than simple constructing comparative figures, since the points at which calculations were made vary in each of the original studies[24] and two studies included sexual offences other than rape or attempted rape (Lees and Gregory, 1993; Jamieson et al., 1998).

All the studies demonstrate that the highest proportion of cases is lost at the earliest stages, with between half and two-thirds dropping out before referral to prosecutors. The rate of 'no criming'[25] remains high, despite repeated guidelines from the Home Office (see, for example, Home Office, 1983) and internally within the police, specifying that it should be confined to false allegations[26], crimes that occurred in another area and/or were recorded as a crime in error (Home Office, 2003). No study has found 'no criming' to be limited to these categories. The most significant factors in early loss of cases are designation as false reports and withdrawals by the victim/complainant.

---

22. This unpublished study was a pilot exploring the feasibility of a large-scale tracking project across Scotland. The sample comprised all sexual offences cases reported in two police areas during 1996-1997, of which a minority were rape. The study concluded that to track all sex offences across the country would prove extremely expensive.
23. Presented at the *Promoting the Model* conference, Manchester, in 1997.
24. Several analyse from a base of 100 per cent at each stage of the legal process, meaning that significant re-calculation has had to be done on the original data.
25. Home Office guidance advises that the police may no-crime a case where following the report of an incident which has subsequently been recorded as a crime, additional verifiable information is available which determines that no notifiable crime has been committed.
26. Defined as either where the complainant makes a clear retraction or where there is strong evidence that the report was false.

Table 3.3: **UK research findings on attrition in reported rape cases[1]**

	Chambers and Millar, 1983*	Grace et al, 1992	Lees and Gregory, 1993[2]	St Mary's 1996-7	Jamieson et al, 1998[2] *	Harris and Grace, 1999	Lea et al, 2003
Initial sample size	196	464	109	378	47	483	379
Police stage							
Cases lost	46%	–	57%	44%	36%	67%	61%
No-crimed	22%	45%	43%	–	–	25%	11%
Unsolved	24%	7%	7%	–	–	11%	–
NFA	–	10%	6%	–	–	31%	–
Prosecution stage							
Referred to CPS	54%	–	43%	30%	64%	31%	–
Discontinued	16%	–	18%	7%	32%	8%	14%
Court stage							
Prosecutions	38%	33%	25%	24%	32%	20%	–
Rape conviction	15%	19%	9%	9%	15%3	6%	5%
Conviction other	10%	8%	2%	–	4%3	7%	6%
Acquittal	9%	7%	14%	–	4%3	7%	–

Notes

1 Studies presented findings in different ways and full data sets were not accessible to perform any re-calculation. Figures are not available, therefore, for each stage of the attrition process, and some data are missing.

2 Data limited to the rape and attempted rape cases in the sample.
   For some cases the outcomes were still unknown.

* Research conducted in Scotland

These studies suggest higher levels of prosecution and conviction in Scotland. However, when national data for rape complaints only are examined, a similar pattern to England and Wales appears, with conviction rates falling year-on-year to six per cent in 2001 (see Figure 3.8). One difference, however, is that a higher percentage (close to 50%) of cases that are prosecuted result in convictions in Scotland.

Figure 3.7:   *Attrition in rape cases in Scotland 1977-2001*

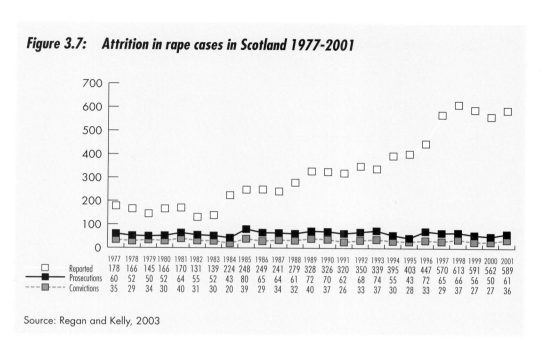

	1977	1978	1979	1980	1981	1982	1983	1984	1985	1986	1987	1988	1989	1990	1991	1992	1993	1994	1995	1996	1997	1998	1999	2000	2001
Reported	178	166	145	166	170	131	139	224	248	249	241	279	328	326	320	350	339	395	403	447	570	613	591	562	589
Prosecutions	60	52	50	52	64	55	52	43	80	65	64	61	72	70	62	68	74	55	43	72	65	66	56	50	61
Convictions	35	29	34	30	40	31	30	20	39	29	34	32	40	37	26	33	37	30	28	33	29	37	27	27	36

Source: Regan and Kelly, 2003

Attrition internationally

In studies of attrition rates across Europe (Kelly and Regan, 2001; Regan and Kelly, 2003), Finland, Ireland and Sweden displayed the same stark trends over time as the UK, in relation to reporting and conviction rates. Whilst a number of other countries recorded variations in reporting, a decline in the proportion of prosecutions and convictions was a common trend for every country that provided data, apart from Germany where the proportion of prosecutions and convictions has risen since 1997. Much higher prosecution rates, for example more than 50 per cent of reports in Austria and Denmark, were evident, alongside a number of countries where the majority of prosecutions resulted in convictions (Finland, Germany, Hungary, Iceland). Overall these data suggest that, whilst some core problems link adversarial and investigative legal systems, a number of European countries have higher prosecution and conviction rates than the UK. In fact, the only country with a lower conviction rate was Ireland (Regan and Kelly, 2003).

Bachman and Paternoster (1993) note the absence of research in the US to address whether the policy intent underlying rape law reform has been reflected in increased reporting and prosecution, especially of rape by known assailants. They conclude, drawing on a range of national data sources, that there has been some impact, but it is not substantial, and that compared with robbery and assault offences there is still a large discrepancy between reported offences and convictions, and a strong 'acquaintance discount', for rape offences. Slightly stronger impacts were found adjusting the methodology and looking at three states (Bachman and Smith, 1994) but the higher attrition rate compared to other serious crimes persisted.

The Senate Judiciary Committee issued a report entitled *Detours on the Road to Equal Justice* in 1993 that documented attrition in rape cases across the USA. The average conviction rate in 1990 was 12 per cent. The report demonstrates disparities in how rape and other violent crimes were prosecuted. The key Attrition points identified were: arrest (62% of reported rapes do not result in an arrest); dismissal (of the cases that moved into the system, 48% were dismissed before trial); and acquittal at trial. The committee also noted reluctance amongst prosecutors to bring cases where the parties were known to one another – the majority of rape cases. However, the review found significantly higher conviction rates in particular areas of the US, including Washington and New York. A subsequent review notes that conviction rates across the USA range from 2.5 to 19.9 per cent (Sinclair and Bourne, 1998, p576) but offered little explanation of these wide discrepancies.

Brereton (1993) discusses four Australian studies where patterns similar to those documented for England and Wales and the USA are reported. The key players are the victim, in terms of the decision to report and continuing with the case, and the police in terms of the decision of whether to lay charges and their influence on the victim's subsequent decision-making. Several studies also note 20 to 35 per cent of cases being dropped by prosecutors. Guilty pleas are much lower than in other criminal cases. Two factors had the most impact on outcomes at trial: evidence of physical injury; and admissions by the defendant at some point in the process.

Identifying Attrition points

Attrition research identifies a paradox internationally: despite widespread reform of statute law and, in many jurisdictions, procedural rules, the 1990s witnessed declining or static conviction rates. The UK has one of the most pronounced patterns. Remarkably little research or legal commentary has, as yet, attempted to explain these common – and unexpected – international similarities.

Research to date in adversarial legal systems has identified four key points at which attrition occurs. The first point is the decision to report itself; estimates of the reporting rate range from 5 to 25 per cent. Even using the highest reporting rate estimate, three-quarters of cases never reach the first hurdle within the CJS. The second involves the police investigation stage – the initial response, forensic examination, statement taking, evidence gathering and arrest and/or interviewing of suspects – between half and three-quarters of reported cases are lost here. The third point relates to the minority of cases that are referred through to prosecutors, where a proportion are discontinued. The final point is the even smaller number of cases that reach court, where between one-third and over one-half of those involving adults result in acquittals. At each of the points the possibility of withdrawal by the victim exists, although the largest number of these occur during the reporting and investigative stages – what the authors term 'early withdrawals'.

This is only part of the story, however, since attrition varies according the characteristics of the case. The most recent studies in England, Wales and Scotland concur that cases involving children are more likely to be prosecuted and to result in convictions. Adult rape cases have higher attrition rates, especially if they depart from the 'real rape' template. Cases involving complainants who have mental health problems or some form of learning disability are rarely prosecuted (Harris and Grace, 1999; Lea et al., 2003). In thinking about Attrition points, it may prove useful to distinguish between cases that are lost and those that are dropped. The latter involves cases where either a police officer or prosecutor makes a clear and explicit decision to not proceed with a case. Cases can be lost in a number of ways: through failure to identify and/or find the assailant; the withdrawal of the victim; and acquittals in court. In the analysis of attrition the authors have sought to highlight both processes and case characteristics to illuminate the many factors at play. Since attempts to reduce attrition should target specific points in the process, it is hoped that a more detailed documentation of how and why cases are lost or dropped will enhance efforts to address the justice gap.

The decision to report

Sexual violence, and rape in particular, is considered the most under-reported crime (American Medical Association, 1995). Whilst a number of studies have explored the reasons for not reporting, the equally significant decision to report has received less attention. In terms of understanding attrition, this is unfortunate, since knowing what women are seeking when they approach the police may offer insights into their subsequent decision-making. The findings below draw on international prevalence studies and a series of 'phone-in' surveys in Australia designed to explore responses of services to reported rape (for more details see Kelly, 2002).

A wide range of reasons for not reporting have been documented, the major ones being:

- not naming the event as rape (and/or 'a crime') oneself[27];
- not thinking the police/others will define the event as rape;

---

27. In BCS data, only 43 per cent of women subject since the age of 16 to an act that met the 1994 legal definition of rape actually thought of it as rape (Walby and Allen, 2004)

- fear of disbelief;
- fear of blame/judgement;
- distrust of the police/courts/legal process;
- fear of family and friends knowing/public disclosure[28];
- fear of further attack/intimidation;
- divided loyalty in cases involving current/ex-intimates; and
- language/communication issues for women with disabilities and/or whose first language is not that of the country where they were assaulted.

For many women it is a combination of factors that militate against reporting and some feature more strongly for certain groups of women than others. A heightened mistrust of the police has been frequently noted, for example, among women from minority ethnic communities (Commission on Women and the Criminal Justice System, 2004).[29] What has received less attention are the heightened concerns about others knowing and fear that they might be blamed (especially, if alcohol or drugs were involved) which disproportionately affect young women. Many of the factors that discourage reporting are connected to the notion of 'real rape': the phone-in survey in Victoria, Australia, for example, notes that almost two-thirds of cases (60%) involving strangers were reported compared to less than one-quarter (21%) of those involving known men (Brereton, 1993); and the BCS data also found (Myhill and Allen, 2002), stranger assaults were more than twice as likely than any other assaults involving any other perpetrator to be reported whereas assaults in the context of 'dates' the least likely.

In the limited studies that ask victims/survivors why they chose to report (see, for example, Jordan, 2001a) the primary reasons are less varied and include:

- acting automatically/it seeming the 'right' thing to do;
- wanting to prevent attacks on others;
- wanting protection for oneself; and
- a desire for justice/redress.

Almost all of the factors identified by research as increasing the likelihood of reporting relate to the elements which constitute 'real rape': that the offender was a stranger; force and injury were involved; and it took place either in a public place or in the context of a break-in. However, there is contradictory research that shows that for England and Wales the proportion of stranger attacks in rapes reported to the police has decreased from 35 per

---

28. Anonymity is not guaranteed in some of the jurisdictions where research has been conducted.
29. Although a number of projects in the USA note high rates of reporting from Black and ethnic minority women (see, for example, Russell, 1984).

cent in 1985 to 12 per cent in 1996 (Harris and Grace, 1999).[30] The only exception is when the person whom the woman first tells about the assault strongly communicates that it is not the woman's fault and supports the idea of reporting to the police (Schwartz, 1997, pxiv).

In terms of the criminal justice system, the issue of 'prompt' (i.e. immediate) reporting continues to be influential, despite the fact that it is no longer officially a form of corroboration. Jordan's (1998) study of women reporting rape in New Zealand shows that the police were the first to be told in only six per cent of cases, and in almost half of the reported cases (46%) someone other than the woman made the initial contact with the police.[31] In the majority of instances this took place with her consent and/or co-operation, but a minority were catapulted into a situation not of their choosing. The BCS data are similar, with 52 per cent of those reporting doing so themselves, in 35 per cent of cases someone else doing so, and in 13 per cent the police finding out some other way (Myhill and Allen, 2002, pvii). Whether having the decision to report made by someone else is a factor in some subsequent decisions to withdraw complaints has yet to be systematically studied.[32]

Expanding the concept of 'real rape'

The data from UK and international research question the presumptions that rape is a single event, committed by strangers. Rape is a more frequent and mundane crime than conventionally believed, with current and ex-partners featuring strongly, and for a substantial proportion of women rape involves repeat victimisation. The power of the 'real rape' template, however, continues to affect how rape is defined and understood by everyone, beginning with victims themselves (Myhill and Allen, 2002). An interesting example from the most recent BCS findings is that less than half (43%) of women who had experienced an assault that met the legal definition of rape defined it as such, and this was even lower where the perpetrator was a current or ex-partner (31%). However, where the assault had led to additional physical injury, the proportion defining it as 'rape' increased markedly to 62 per cent (Walby and Allen, 2004). The irony of low levels of reporting by current partners is illustrated by Bergen's (1995) qualitative study, which demonstrates that

---

30. A more recent study (Lea et al., 2003) and this report's data (see later sections) found a less marked decrease in the proportion of assaults by strangers.

31. This is similar to a Scottish study (Chambers and Millar, 1983): in 40 per cent of cases someone other than the victim made the decision to report, and 17 per cent would have preferred the police not to have been told. The interviews with victims in the study also revealed that only 29 per cent made the decision to report entirely alone.

32. The ability to explore this issue was compromised by the CPS asking that a series of questions on who the complainant first told and their response be removed from the questionnaire, in order to prevent the research tools being deemed disclosable in any cases that went to court.

'marital rape' is often extremely brutal, with one-third being termed 'sadistic', and the majority of women being raped 'frequently' i.e. more than 20 times. Only one-third defined these incidents as rape at the time, and only half of this group immediately separated. Re-definition occurred when: the assaults reached a level of brutality associated with stranger rape; the woman accessed support; and/or she separated. Overlaps between rape and domestic violence have received limited attention in either research or policy development (an exception is Walby and Allen, 2004). This overlap however clearly deserves greater exploration, not least with respect to the protection issues victims may need addressing in order to sustain a prosecution, and the finding that women who kill abusive partners are much more likely to have been subjected to repeated sexual violence (see, for example, Jones, 1980).

Summary

- Home Office data on reported rape cases in England and Wales show a continuing and unbroken increase in reporting to the police over the past two decades, but a relatively static number of convictions, thus the increasing justice gap.
- Prosecuted cases involving children were more likely to result in conviction than those involving adults.
- All UK studies of attrition in rape cases concur that the highest proportion of cases are lost at the earliest stages, with between half and two-thirds dropping out at the investigative stage, and withdrawal by complainants one of the most important elements.
- A number of studies have found high rates of 'no criming', not limited to the official guidelines for this category.
- Research on attrition in Europe shows that a decline in the proportion of prosecutions and convictions was a common trend, although only Ireland had a lower conviction rate than the UK.
- Research to date has identified four key points at which attrition occurs: the decision to report itself; the police investigative stage; discontinuance by prosecutors; and at trial. Victim withdrawals can occur at each stage but the highest proportion is evident at the first two points.

4.   Understanding attrition: the research findings

This chapter seeks to strengthen the knowledge base on the processes involved in attrition, especially with respect to early withdrawal by complainants.

The authors begin by outlining the attrition process in the study sample, firstly (see Table 4.1) according to the categories used by the police and most previous studies of attrition: 'no crime'; undetected; detected no proceedings; and detected. The detected cases that are proceeded with then appear under CPS prosecution and trial. The range of the research data and the prospective design means it has been possible to develop a more detailed set of categories that explicate the complex and varied reasons behind the official designations. These categories are: no evidence of assault; false allegation; insufficient evidence; no prospect of conviction; victim declines to complete initial process; and victim withdrawal (see Table 4.2). The first four reflect police decision-making (often in liaison with CPS) and the latter two actions taken by the complainant. The difference between 'insufficient evidence' and 'no prospect of conviction' is the extent of CPS involvement. 'Victim declines to complete initial process' covers cases where the complainant chooses not to make an official complaint, give a statement and/or have a forensic examination, as well as those where the complainant did not respond to early police efforts to make contact.[33] Withdrawals are defined as cases where these initial processes take place and support for the case is withdrawn – sometimes within days of the report being made. Both constitute this report's original category of 'early withdrawals'.

Subsequent sections deal with a series of 'Attrition points' revealed by this analysis, which follow a roughly chronological order of the criminal justice process. In Attrition point 1, which focuses on the decision to report to the police, findings are based on the full case-tracking sample of 3,527 cases, i.e. both unreported and reported cases; analysis from Attrition point 2 onwards is based only on cases reported to the police.

For each Attrition point key factors contributing to cases being lost or not proceeding are identified, bringing to bear a range of relevant project data. Three elements of the data, in

---

33. Originally, the term 'non co-operation with the prosecution' was used, but during analysis it was realised that this represented a police perspective, rather than a more open possibility that it could be personal factors or system failures that accounted for the actions of the complainant. It was the following passage from an interview, which led to this reconsideration: *"I just was really, really angry. And, somehow it's not acceptable for you to be like that. Because even in dealings with the police you're expected to be courteous and to be co-operative, this is what I feel is the expectation of you as the victim, to be co-operative"* (St Mary's, Service User Interview 11, Undetected).

particular, provide a window in to the complex decision-making processes of both complainants and criminal justice professionals in rape cases: the case-tracking database; pro formas completed by police officers on case progress and outcomes; and the questionnaires from and interviews with complainants. Extended quotes from the interviewees have been used in places to convey a sense of the complexities involved and, either the context in which they are making decisions or how the responses of the CJS are perceived. Interview material from SARC staff and police officers is also drawn on where relevant. The primary interest was to explore the early attrition process, which has been less researched than stages involving the CPS and trial, so whilst data on ultimate outcomes are presented, the most detailed analysis concentrates on earlier stages. The data which follow offer some support to those who have been critical of the investigative and prosecution processes, whilst also illuminating the less than simple challenges and dilemmas facing police, CPS and, ultimately, government about how to investigate, assess and classify cases.

The attrition process

Using police designations and the entire data-set, more than one-fifth of reported cases (22%, n=575) were 'no crimed' and one-third (33%, n=882) were undetected. Just under one-third (30%, n=787) had been detected, but in 12 per cent of cases (n=320) no proceedings were brought. In a further one-fifth of cases (15%, n=399) there was not complete information on case outcomes, either because the police failed to complete pro formas or the case was not concluded at the end of the research. Additionally, there were a small number of self-referrals who had reported at an earlier point but it was not possible to ascertain precisely when, or what the case outcome was, as well as a small number of cases that were being investigated in a difference police force area.

Table 4.1 presents these data in summary form, calculated in the same way as the Harris and Grace (1999) study – looking separately at the investigative and prosecution processes – for the three SARCs and amalgamated Comparison areas. Cases where the police designation (n=339) or CPS decision (n=60) is missing in the data have been excluded here, reducing the sample to a total of 2,244 cases, and hence, changing the percentages noted above.

Table 4.1: Case outcomes for 2,244 cases reported to the police where police/CPS decision known

	St Mary's		REACH		STAR		Comparison		All	
	N	%	N	%	N	%	N	%	N	%
Police investigation										
No Crime	233	27%	82	31%	207	26%	53	17%	575	26%
Undetected	294	34%	90	34%	324	40%	174	57%	882	39%
Detected	343	39%	91	35%	274	34%	79	26%	787	35%
Detected no/not proceeding	146	17%	35	13%	90	11%	49	16%	320	14%
Total	870	100%	263	100%	805	100%	306	100%	2244	100%
CPS/Trial										
Cautioned	2	1%	-	-%	5	3%	2	7%	9	2%
Victim withdrawal	23	12%	3	5%	12	7%	2	7%	40	9%
Discontinued	17	9%	8	14%	34	18%	-	-%	59	13%
Pending trial	29	15%	7	13%	19	10%	17	57%	72	15%
Acquittal	49	25%	18	32%	36	20%	1	3%	104	22%
Conviction	77	39%	20	36%	78	42%	8	27%	183	39%
Total	197	100%	56	100%	184	100%	30	100%	467	100%
Conviction as percentage of reported cases		9%		8%		10%		3%		8%

Source: case-tracking database

The first point to highlight is that the conviction rate is higher for this sample than the national averages for 2001 and 2002. This is accounted for by the fact that two of the SARC areas (St Mary's and STAR) had higher conviction rates, and represent two-thirds of cases in the sample.[34] This provides some limited data suggesting that SARCs can make a contribution to decreasing attrition.

In order to examine the reasons for cases not proceeding within the different police classifications ('no crime', undetected and detected no proceedings), the outcomes for all 2,643 cases reported to the police in the case-tracking database were collated using a combination of the police and authors' categories (these are presented separately for each site in Appendix 5). This analysis reveals the continued inconsistency in police allocations, with cases for each of the categories appearing under all the police designations.

A salient example is the 'no crime' category, which, as documented in previous studies, continues to be used for a far wider group of cases than counting rules designate. Over one in five of all reported cases in the sample (22%, n=575 of 2,643) were recorded by police as 'no crimes', rising to more than one in four (26%, n=575 of 2,244) of those where the police classification was known (see Table 4.1). Whilst officially this category should be limited to a narrow range of circumstances (recorded in error, where the offence took place in another jurisdiction, where there is credible evidence that no offence took place), it still functions as something of a 'dustbin'. There are a proportion of reports in the sample that were made in other jurisdictions, both in the UK and abroad, and whilst the latter is not problematic, the former raises the possibility that some reports (n=36 in our sample) are being counted twice, if official figures include 'no crimes'. The credible evidence that no offence took place includes what the authors have called 'no evidence of assault' and cases designated as false allegations, the latter representing just under one-third (30%, n=175) of 'no crimes'. However, false allegations also appear under several other headings. A further 37 false allegations appear under other classifications at the police stage (29 as undetected and 8 as detected no proceedings), while there are four where the classification was unknown.

Other obvious anomalies in the 'no crime' category include: cases designated 'no crime' when the reason for no further action is that a) there has been a victim withdrawal, b) the case is dropped because the victim is ill or especially vulnerable, c) there is insufficient

---

34. The least unknown outcomes were for STAR, due to the case-tracking element of their service provision, and for the Comparison groups, where Project Sapphire provided much appreciated assistance in the final stages of data analysis in chasing up case outcomes. It is, therefore, possible that the conviction rates in the St Mary's and REACH areas are higher still, since the 'outcome unknown' category by definition contains some cases that were proceeding to trial, but for which the eventual outcome is not yet known.

evidence or d) the suspect has not been found or identified. The 'no crime' category comprises a complex layering of different kinds of cases and circumstances, many of which are not 'false' in the literal meaning of this term. Clearly, neither victim withdrawals nor cases where there is insufficient evidence should be included as 'no crimes'. Cases were also wrongly designated 'undetected' when there was a) a named suspect, b) a suspect had been arrested and was on police bail, and c) when an advice file had been submitted to the CPS. The ability of the Home Office, or even local police forces, to monitor attrition is severely undermined by such inconsistency in basic data entry.

The attrition process revisited

Earlier, Table 4.1 presented all cases in the case-tracking sample that were reported to the police in the SARC and Comparison areas where police and CPS decisions were known (n=2,244). In Table 4.2 aggregated data for all areas are presented using the categories which afford a more detailed examination of the attrition process. Cases with missing data at the police (n=299) and CPS stages (n=60) are, again, removed, making a base sample of 2,284.[35] Analysis using both sets of categories in combination is presented for each individual research sites in Appendix 5.

In the following sections there are more detailed discussions of the most significant Attrition points evident in this sample of over 2,000 cases. These roughly, although not exactly, follow the points in time at which decisions are made in order to focus on the early stages of the process, which previous studies, along with this study, confirm are the points at which most cases are lost/dropped. This section of the report concludes by combining categories across the time periods and exploring whether there were any factors associated with a conviction. The influences at play in terms of attrition at each stage can be multiple and may be specific to an individual case, however, triangulation of the case-tracking data, service user questionnaires and interviews enables identification of some of the most important factors.

Summary

- Around one-quarter of reported cases were 'no crimed'.
- Just under one-third of reported cases were detected but in a notable proportion of these no proceedings were brought.

---

35. There is a slight discrepancy between the sample sizes in Tables 4.1 and 4.2 due to the different categories reported on at the police stage. In Table 4.1 all cases where the police classification was known were included, whereas in Table 4.2 the authors report on the reason for the case not proceeding. There are a number of additional cases here, because while it was known that the case did not proceed and the reason why, the police classification was not known and therefore could not be included in Table 4.1.

Table 4.2: **Recalculated Attrition process: 2,284 cases reported to police where research categories known**

n=2,284	No	%	Overall %
Police	*1,817*	*100%*	*80%*
Insufficient evidence	386	21	
Victim withdrawal	318	17	
Victim declined to complete initial process	315	17	
Offender not identified	239	13	
False allegation	216	12	
No evidence of assault	83	5	
No prospect conviction	37	2	
Not in public interest	20	1	
Other	67	4	
Reason unknown	136	8	
CPS	*145*	*100%*	*6%*
Caution/final reprimand	9	6	
Discontinued	38	26	
Victim withdrawal	25	17	
Suspect fled prior to PDH	1	1	
Pending trial	72	50	
Trial	*322*	*100%*	*14%*
Trial to be rearranged, suspect fled	1	<1	
Victim withdrawal	15	5	
Discontinued/withdrawn at court	19	6	
Acquittal	104	32	
Guilty plea	89	28	
Not clear if guilty plea/conviction	17	5	
Part conviction	11	3	
Conviction	66	20	
Total convictions	183		8%

Source: case-tracking database

- A conviction rate of eight per cent was found across the research sites collectively, although this was slightly higher for two of the individual SARC sites.
- This is higher than the national average of 5.6 per cent.

- Inconsistencies were found in the police classification of case outcomes, particularly in the 'no crime' category.
- Eighty per cent of cases did not proceed beyond the police stage, with a further 6 per cent being discontinued by the CPS, and only 14 per cent proceeding to trial.

Attrition point 1: reporting to the police

This section explores the decision-making of complainants at the earliest stage of the process – reporting rape/sexual assault to the police. Using the case-tracking database comparative analysis was conducted between reported and unreported cases across a range of variables, to see whether there were particular characteristics associated with either group. The service user questionnaire and interview data provide additional insights into the range of routes by which the decision to report is arrived at and how soon after the attack reports are made.

The decision to report

Of the 3,172 victims/survivors who contacted the three SARCs during the evaluation period, 2,288 (72% of all cases) reported to the police. In the Comparison areas all cases (n=355) were, by definition, reported to the police, making a total of 2,643 reported cases from all sites. A proportion of self-referrals to the SARCs are seeking support and information about historic abuse, but the majority relate to recent assaults (for discussion of the differences between police and self-referrals see Lovett et al., 2004). A further factor is a small number of cases where the assault took place in another country whilst on holiday or business. Although 13 per cent (n=96) of self-referrals had a forensic medical examination, only a small proportion of this group (n=13, all from St Mary's) went on to make an official police report.[36] Among the self-referrals, there is therefore, a discernible group of women and men making a clear decision to avoid the CJS, whilst seeking the health checks and other support and advice they need to cope with the recent sexual victimisation.

Analysis of the case-tracking database was undertaken comparing the 2,643 cases who reported to the police with the 884 cases who did not. The key findings are summarised here.

- Reporting decreases with age: 90 per cent (n=355) of under-16s reported, compared with 72 per cent (n=581) of those aged 26 to 35 and 69 per cent (n=458) of those aged 36 and over. However, where details were known, there was far more reporting by a 'known other' (56%, n=96) than by the victim/survivor themselves for under-16s.

36. Another small group of cases reported some time prior to attending the SARC (n=16; St Mary's n=5, STAR n=11).

- A slightly higher proportion of women than men reported to the police (75%, n=2,474 compared with 69%, n=169).
- The majority of cases where the complainant had a disability (88%, n=170) or was involved in prostitution (97%, n=66) were reported.[37]
- Assaults by known perpetrators were the least likely to be reported (75%, n=1,369) compared with the highest rate of reporting for assaults by recent acquaintances (88%, n=297).

A larger proportion of the sub-sample of questionnaire respondents and interviewees (82%, n=188 and 77%, n=43 respectively) had made a report to the police. Analysis of these data provides insights into additional factors influencing the decision to report to the police that escape quantitative analysis. The main reasons respondents gave (n=178 who answered the question, multiple responses possible) were:

- to sanction the perpetrator (69%, n=122);
- to protect others (57%, n=101);
- because they thought they should (50%, n=89); and
- fear of the perpetrator (44%, n=79).

Where known (n=179), just under half (46%, n=83) made the report themselves, most commonly by telephone, and three-quarters (76%, n=136 of 188) said that they made the decision to report.

The 40 respondents who did not report to the police provided a range of reasons for their decision. The most common were:

- the abuse took place some time ago (n=5);
- concern about not being believed (n=5);
- not wanting others to know (n=4);
- lack of faith in the police (n=4);
- confusion (n=4);
- relationship to the offender (n=4); and
- not being able to face the criminal justice process (n=3).

Therefore, for a significant proportion of this group lack of faith in aspects of the criminal justice system acted as a deterrent to reporting.

---

37. This might indicate limited awareness of the possibility of self-referral amongst these groups.

Timing of the report

Whilst prompt reporting no longer functions as a form of legally required corroboration, and is now understood as telling anyone and not just confined to making an official report, delays in reporting continue to influence the perceptions of police and prosecutors. This study has already cited research showing that: a) police are rarely the first people to be told; b) the importance of the response of those who are told first in determining whether the case will be reported and c) that reports immediately following assaults are the exception rather than the rule. Figure 4.1 presents findings on the length of time between the assault and the reporting to the police, and shows that around half were reported within six hours (54%, n=784) and four out of five within 24 hours (79%, n=1150).

Figure 4.1:   Length of time between the assault and reporting to police

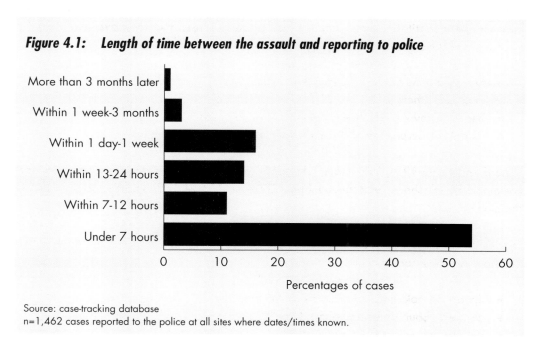

Percentages of cases

Source: case-tracking database
n=1,462 cases reported to the police at all sites where dates/times known.

Cross-tabulations were conducted within the case-tracking database to see whether there was any correlation between these time intervals and relationship with the perpetrator in cases involving a single assailant. Unsurprisingly, the vast majority of those assaulted by recent acquaintances and strangers reported within 24 hours (87%, n=155 of 179 recent acquaintances and 85%, n=347 of 398 strangers). However, high proportions of ex- and current partner cases were also reported within this period (74%, n=84 of 113 ex-partners and 66%, n=70 of 106 current partners). These proportions also held for reports made within 12 hours.

Questionnaire respondents reflected these reporting patterns, with over half of reports (58%, n=105 of 180 where details known) being made within 12 hours of the assault and almost three-quarters (70%, n=126) within 24 hours. Those who had delayed reporting for more than 12 hours attributed this to some combination of shock, fear, confusion or distress. For a small number the confusion related to whether, in fact, anything had happened and this was particularly the case where the respondent thought that they had been drugged.

The following accounts from interviewees illustrate the multiple routes to reporting, why delays of more than 24 hours are not only quite common, but also entirely understandable, and the role of others – both in making reports and/or encouraging them.

> I did, but I did it 24 hours later, 'cause of the two kids, well, not just because of them, I just didn't know what to do...They sent a WPC just to talk to me, and then the CID woman, I still am annoyed by her. She sort of just barged in ... "Right, come on, we're going to St Mary's, going to the police station." And I didn't want my little girl to know. She's only five ... she was adamant that I had to get someone to mind them, which I did ... the WPC was great, you know, she [CID] was talking to me and but she just sort of took control, because I hadn't even made up my mind whether I did want to press charges or even do anything about it really, but she just sort of seemed to make me do it. (St Mary's, Service User Interview 3, Undetected)

> Well actually, I didn't report, I thought I was to blame. It's quite simple. I'd gone out and stayed out longer than expected, I'd had enough to drink to know that I needed a little help to get home. I needed somebody to get me a taxi, put me in it, and then I could have got home. So I was tipsy, but not drunk. And this gentleman said he would look after me, and I asked him could I trust him? And he said yes. He brought me home, on the tram, which I'd never been on before ... We got to my house, and ... at the door, I stretched my arm and said, "I'll get you a taxi." I didn't invite him in. But the next thing, as I'm phoning for the taxi, I realised he was sat on the settee. Then I was raped, and then he went. I felt a stupid old woman, because I'm fifty-odd ... But I felt as though I could trust him ... I wasn't going to tell anybody because I felt so ashamed, and I felt as though it was my fault ... Anyway, she [neighbour] came in the day after, and she just looked at me, and she said, "You look shocking, tell me what's the matter." "If I told you what's the matter," I said, "You'll never speak to me again" ... I felt so dirty, even though I'd showered, showered, showered and washed and washed – but fortunately I hadn't washed the clothes or the bedding. Anyway, she was asking me questions, had I been assaulted, had I been mugged, and I said "No, no, no," and then she just turned round and she said, "Have you been raped?"

Well then I broke down … And she said, "You know what you've got to do." I said, "I can't." She said, "Well I am. I will." And she phoned the police.

(St Mary's, Service User Interview 10, Acquittal)

I was away from home, on a residential weekend as part of a course, so, you know, apart from one friend there, my family weren't with me, and it was people I knew so I was really shocked, so I didn't report it to the police for a few days. I find people don't understand this unless they've been through it, because, especially when it's people you know, and also there was drugs involved so I had a couple of hours of the assault which I couldn't remember … So I had trouble believing it myself at first … I really didn't know what to do, I didn't know the centre at St Mary's existed, the only thing I thought of at first was I spoke to a friend at home and she said, "What about ringing one of these Rape Crisis Centres, somewhere like that?" I was just too exhausted emotionally, I'd been physically sick and I was, you know, crying most of the time and I just didn't have the energy to deal with it or to make any decision. I came home, I was very strange, I was sat home for the day before I told my husband, and he wanted me to go to the police and then I got frightened because it became an issue of control and I couldn't think straight, I needed to know that I was doing what I needed to do and not what other people told me to do. I booked an appointment with my doctor … I've had sort of post-natal depression and also clinical depression over the years, and I trusted her … she said I should see St Mary's … St Mary's said that if they did a forensic examination, none of the tests would go anywhere unless I involved the police. And I thought, "Well what's the point?" … I don't want to just be examined for no purpose … I didn't realise that I wouldn't get any answers anyway, but that's beside the point.

(St Mary's, Service User Interview 11, Undetected)

There were a couple of reasons [why I didn't report it]: at first, I couldn't face it. I thought that I would eventually, but because my husband was actually, I think, mentally ill before this happened, and quite distressed, and he became very difficult afterwards, I got more sort of concerned with his health than mine. And it seemed that things were difficult enough without facing anything even bigger … What I would have liked to have done, was to give all the information – 'cause I knew who the man was – but not to have to have an interview. I would have liked to have written it down and handed it over and said, "Look, there's the information, I'm sorry but I can't face being questioned or being in court or anything else, but just for your information, this was it." And I did eventually ring a police station to ask if it was possible to give a name but not be involved, and what I was told was that they couldn't guarantee it … So that put me off … I felt all along my husband wasn't so much thinking about what was right for me, it was for him.

(REACH, Service User Interview 4, Unreported)

Summary

- 72 per cent of referrals to the SARCs and 75 per cent of the sample overall reported to the police.
- Reports to the police were more likely with respect to younger complainants and those with disabilities or involved in prostitution.
- Assaults by known perpetrators were the least likely to be reported and those by recent acquaintances the most likely.
- The most common reasons questionnaire respondents gave for reporting were: to sanction the perpetrator; to protect others; they thought they should; and fear of the perpetrator.
- The most common reasons given by those who did not report were: the abuse took place some time ago; fear of not being believed; and concerns about elements of the CJS process.
- Where reports to the police were made, around half were within six hours and the majority within 24 hours of the assault. The nature of the relationship with the perpetrator had limited effect on the promptness of reporting.

Attrition point 2: no evidence of assault and false allegations

This section addresses two groups of cases that did not proceed beyond a very early stage – those where, according to the police, there was no evidence of an assault taking place and those designated as false allegations. Findings on the former are drawn solely from the police pro formas, while three perspectives on false allegations are provided by analysis of: the case-tracking database, the police pro formas, and interviews with police officers and SARC staff.

No evidence of assault

A group of cases not addressed in previous studies are those where there is, what has been termed in this study ,'no evidence of assault' (n=83). Police pro formas provided sufficient detail for more in-depth analysis on 56 of these cases (far more were evident in the St Mary's data, n=35), of which there were two distinct types. The first type is when there is no complaint of rape from the individual (see also Jordan 2001a): in 12 of these cases at the point the police made contact the individual was either too drunk or distressed to communicate, the presence of injuries or torn clothing led to an initial coding of 'suspected rape', but as soon as the person was able to provide an account it became clear that this was not what took place; for a further 11 the complaint was made by someone other than the supposed victim (often a family member or partner) and the initial investigation revealed that no sexual offence had taken place. There is a larger group of 31 cases

(28 women and 3 men) where people regain consciousness – either in a public place or at home – with no memory of the previous time period. They approach the police because they are worried that they may have been assaulted whilst asleep, unconscious or affected by alcohol or drugs. In every such case police reported that the ensuing forensic examination (and in some cases toxicology tests) suggested no sex had taken place and the individuals were reported as being relieved by this. Clearly 'no crime' really did take place in many of these situations. It is, however, an open question whether this group of cases should be combined with false allegations in police record-keeping. This is for two reasons: firstly 'no evidence of assault' is not a contested category; and secondly, given the data presented later on how 'previous allegations' undermine the credibility of complainants, there is a danger that such records might in the future be read, erroneously, in this way.[38]

False allegations

False allegations have been one of the most contested areas within law enforcement responses to rape, with research suggesting rates are no higher than for other crimes sitting alongside perceptions of police officers and the media who take the opposite view. Some of the most frequently cited US studies put the rate as low as two per cent (Katz and Mazur, 1979).

There were 216 cases classified as false allegations: as a proportion of all 2,643 cases reported to the police this amounts to 8 per cent; as a proportion of the 1,817 cases not proceeding beyond the police stage it is 12 per cent (see Table 4.2). In only six of these cases was there evidence of anyone being arrested, and in only two cases were charges laid, although there were at least 39 named suspects. Six advice files were submitted to CPS, with respect to possible charges being laid against the complainant for perverting the course of justice, and two were charged. Interestingly, most cases in this category had a forensic examination (82%, n=178), whilst far fewer made a formal statement to the police (58%, n=126), suggesting that this is a critical stage for the admission or designation of allegations as false.

Cross-tabulations using the case-tracking database comparing the group designated false allegations (n=216) with proceeding cases (n=527) revealed the following findings.

- Cases involving 16- to 25-year-olds accounted for a higher proportion of cases designated false (52%, n=112) than of cases that proceeded (42%, n=221).
- Those in full-time work formed a smaller proportion of those whose cases were designated false (11%, n=23 compared with 17%, n=91 of those proceeding), whilst the opposite was the case for those who were unemployed (37%, n=79 compared with 18%, n=95).

38. The same argument would apply to cases in the previous section, where there was no complaint from the victim/survivor themselves.

- Whilst small numbers, those with a disability were almost twice as likely to be in the false allegations group as the non-disabled (51%, n=24 of 47 compared with 28%, n=192 of 695), and in 19 of these cases mental health and learning difficulties were present.
- Only 2 of the 66 women involved in prostitution who reported were in the false allegations group.
- A greater degree of acquaintance between victim and perpetrator decreased the likelihood of cases being designated false.
- Cases were more likely to be designated false where previous allegations had been made and/or the complainant had attended the SARC or reported to police in the Comparison areas on a previous occasion.

Exploring the grounds on which cases were deemed to be false allegations is revealing and 120 pro formas contained explanations: in 53 cases the police stated that the complainant admitted the complaint was false, most commonly within days of the initial accusation; 28 cases involved retractions; three non co-operation and in 56 cases the decision was made by the police on evidential grounds. Interestingly, the majority of cases in which the complainant themselves admitted the allegation was false could be categorised as the often quoted motives of 'revenge' (n=8) and 'cover-up' (n=25). Although, as the explanations provided on the police pro formas which are summarised in Box A, reveals, the terms 'revenge' and 'cover up' do not do justice to the complexity of the circumstances involved.

Box A:	Examples of false allegations admitted to by complainants
'Revenge'	'Cover up'
Against a difficult neighbour.	Eight cases of hiding consensual sex with another man from husbands/partners.
Against an ex-partner who the woman had sex with hoping this indicated reconciliation, whilst he had no intention of leaving his new partner.	Nine cases of avoiding confrontations with parents.
Against an ex-partner who had forced sex on previous occasions, although not on this one.	Four cases where accusations arose where the complainant was being investigated for fraud or theft.
To make an ex-partner feel sorry for her.	One case of an affair with a father-in-law.
Against a man who the women had sex with who ignored her the next day.	

There were other unusual contexts, including a young Asian woman who made an accusation as a strategy to prevent her family taking her to Pakistan for an arranged marriage, a young woman wanting the morning after pill after having had unprotected sex and another attempting to regain her mother's support after being thrown out of the family home. In most of these cases there was no named assailant.

Whilst not all of the cases where the complainant 'admitted' making a false allegation can be taken at face value, many of the accounts provided on the police pro formas had a surface credibility. There is, however, considerably less certainty about some of the reasons underpinning police decision-making: 23 refer to mental health problems, 23 to previous allegations (some overlap occurs here); and 13 refer to alcohol and drugs. Evidence from other witnesses that supported the account of the accused was noted in nine cases (two of these involved an alibi), and the absence of CCTV evidence supporting the complainant's account in a further nine cases.[39]

Inconsistencies in the account given by the complainant feature strongly in 30 cases, and in only 5 of these did police officers note that this involved deliberate untruths (lies as opposed to not revealing the whole truth). Previous studies have highlighted the ways in which withholding, or not remembering, information is the outcome of fearing disbelief, which may subsequently be interpreted by police officers and prosecutors as 'lying'.

> Fearing disbelief and judgement, victims of rape may try to embellish their accounts, or conceal wrong-doing, in order to make themselves appear more 'believable' to the police.   (Jordan, 2001a, p93)

> [P]olice scepticism promoted the narration of the very inaccuracies which, in turn, consolidated the police view that women fabricate complaints and make false allegations.   (Chambers and Millar, 1983, pp86-7)

Reflecting this, a number (23%, n=14) of police officers interviewed for this study raised the issue of inconsistencies, and indicated that this had implications for the perceived genuineness of complainants.

> In theory, I would say that somebody who has been raped is going to stick quite rigidly to the account that they give, and that might be an account they give to a uniform police officer and then to us and then perhaps the doctor as well ... whereas

---

39. These were in almost all cases where the complainant claimed to have been in a particular location, often the city/town centre, at a certain time and the CCTV recordings did not confirm this.

sometimes those that have made a false allegation, the story may well change and sometimes they might come out and say things that you know couldn't be possible ... or CCTV might disprove it.   (Comparison 1, Police Officer, DC, F14, July 2002)

The data on the pro formas limit the extent to which one can assess the police designations, but their internal rules on false complaints specify that this category should be limited to cases where either there is a clear and credible admission by the complainants, or where there are strong evidential grounds. On this basis, and bearing in mind the data limitations, for the cases where there is information (n=144) the designation of false complaint could be said to be probable (primarily those where the account by the complainant is referred to) in 44 cases, possible (primarily where there is some evidential basis) in a further 33 cases, and uncertain (including where victim characteristics are used to impute that they are inherently less believable) in 77 cases. If the proportion of false complaints on the basis of the probable and possible cases are recalculated, rates of three per cent are obtained, both of all reported cases (n=67 of 2,643), and of those where the outcome is known (n=67 of 2,284). Even if all those designated false by the police were accepted (a figure of approximately ten per cent), this is still much lower than the rate perceived by police officers interviewed in this study. A question asked of all of them was how they assessed truth and falsity in allegations and within this, 50 per cent (n=31) further discussed the issue of false allegations.

I do deal with a lot of allegations that don't go anywhere, because it transpires that it's not quite a rape, certainly with juveniles. They're in a difficult position, because they scream "Rape," they tell Mother and Father, and before you know it the whole circus has turned out. And then I think it's very difficult for them to say, "Well, it didn't quite happen like that, actually – it was like this" ... It's the same with some adults as well, they've been out, had a good night, got drunk, done something they shouldn't have done, they're married, and they've got to go home and – and then they scream "Rape" and they ruin it for the genuine ones. I don't think that people who make false allegations should be penalised, because clearly there's something wrong, for them to make this allegation, I don't think that's the right way to deal with it ... we spend a lot of time dealing with allegations of rape that really aren't rape, that take a lot of time up. I would say a good half that come through are not genuine ones.
(St Mary's, Police Officer DC, F8, March 2003)

We have a lot of allegations that are then retracted, we have a lot of allegations that it comes out in the wash one way or another that it was consensual. He says it's consensual and she doesn't, or they've been together for like hours beforehand, she's gone back to his flat ... But stranger rape, you immediately start to think "Oh God, this could be a real proper sort of drag you in the car," absolutely nothing beforehand's happened. I think subconsciously you would consider it more serious ... I think I'd have more belief in the victim, that was saying it was by a stranger, that ... it was a proper rape, rather than perhaps someone who said "It's my ex-boyfriend, he came round", 'cause then you start to think things like "Oh, she's just getting back at him now." (St Mary's, Police Officer DC, F2, July 2002)

Well, honestly, it's because most of them are not telling the truth ... I think what happens to a lot of adults is they may have consensual sex with somebody, they get found out by their husband, partner, whoever, they then say "Oh but I didn't consent" as a way of getting themselves out of that trouble ... I mean I have dealt with hundreds and hundreds of rapes in the last few years, and I can honestly probably count on both hands the ones that I believe are truly genuine. (Comparison 1, Police Officer DC, M2, June 2002)

The forensic nurse at St Mary's also illustrates how embedded a tendency to disbelieve complaints is within the police.

One of the things that comes up, time and time again, is their automatic disbelief of a complainant. I'd be getting details off the officer, and they'd say 'Ooh, so what did they say to you in there? What do you think's happened? Sounds a bit dodgy to me' ... It seems to be a natural cynicism, and I am sure that along the way they have met complainants who have made false allegations. It seems to me that everybody then suffers because they happen to have met one or two or maybe more who've told lies... I think they disbelieve – apart from what ... fits their stereotype of a rape, perhaps stranger or the injuries or definitely if she was beaten to a pulp ... I admit it is a difficult crime to prove. But I think the way in which people are handled can always be improved on. They don't know, they weren't there, they should treat that person with respect. I don't see what's so difficult about that. I think even if it's not happened, they're more likely to get a complainant being honest about that much quicker if they're treated the right way, the way any of us would want to be treated. (St Mary's, Forensic nurse, F1, November 2001)

The interviews with police officers and complainants' responses show that despite the focus on victim care, a culture of suspicion remains within the police, even amongst some of those who are specialists in rape investigations. There is also a tendency to conflate false allegations with retractions and withdrawals, as if in all such cases no sexual assault occurred. This reproduces an investigative culture in which elements that might permit a designation of a false complaint are emphasised (later sections reveal how this also feeds into withdrawals and designation of 'insufficient evidence'), at the expense of a careful investigation, in which the evidence collected is evaluated. These perceptions and orientations are not lost on complainants.

Reflections

International research contains salutary lessons about the ease with which cases are dismissed as 'false'. In her analysis of 164 police files in New Zealand, Jordan (2001b) found 3 cases that had been designated false, which subsequently turned out to be early reports of serial rapists. In one of these, a young woman, who was discounted since she was on the fringe of a gang and had minor criminal convictions, named a rapist, who subsequently went on to commit at least 45 stranger rapes over 13 years.[40] One police officer involved in this case reflected on what it had taught him.

> *So the key issue for me is corroboration, to a lesser, a much lesser extent, is credibility. Because professional women get attacked, prostitutes get attacked, people who have been abused previously get attacked, people with criminal convictions get sexually attacked ... You've got to be so careful because sometimes you get discrepancies from genuine complaints too. It's only going through all the evidence, really, and what supports it and what doesn't.* (Jordan, 2001b, pp268, 270)

Summary

- There is a small group of cases, initially treated as rape where there is no evidence of an assault: primarily where a third party makes the report and the victim subsequently denies; or where the victim suspects being assaulted while asleep, unconscious or affected by alcohol/drugs but the medical/forensic examination suggests no sex has taken place. How the police should designate such cases is problematic.
- Eight per cent of reported cases in the sample were designated false by the police.
- A higher proportion of cases designated false involved 16- to 25-year-olds.
- A greater degree of acquaintance between victim and perpetrator decreased the likelihood of cases being designated false.

---

40. The cold case review team in Project Sapphire are apparently encountering similar patterns in London (personal communication, 2004).

- Cases were most commonly designated false on the grounds of: the complainant admitting it; retractions; evidential issues; and non co-operation by the complainant.
- In a number of cases the police also cited mental health problems, previous allegations, use of alcohol/drugs and lack of CCTV evidence.
- The pro formas and the interviews with police officers suggested inconsistencies in the complainant's account could be interpreted as 'lying'.
- The authors' analysis suggests that the designation of false allegations in a number of cases was uncertain according to Home Office counting rules, and if these were excluded, would reduce the proportion of false complaints to three per cent of reported cases.
- This is considerably lower than the estimates of police officers interviewed.

Attrition point 3: insufficient evidence

In this section the different kinds of cases that fail to move beyond the police investigation for evidential reasons are looked at. The largest proportion of cases dropped at the police stage is on the grounds of 'insufficient evidence' (21%, n=386). Two additional groups of cases where lack of evidence is an issue are included in the discussion below: those where no offender was identified (13%, n=239) and those where there was 'no prospect of a conviction' (2%, n=37). In combination these total 662 cases that did not proceed because of evidential difficulties. Two key data sources provide perspectives on these groups of cases: police pro formas, which illustrate the range of issues at play for investigating police officers; and interviews with complainants, which in some cases provide an alternative narrative of the conduct of investigation process.

Analysis of the police pro formas enable the identification of a range of reasons why cases are lost at the investigative stage, including:

- the inability of the complainant to provide a clear account of what happened;
- failure to identify the assailant;
- failure to trace a named assailant;
- assessments by the police (often in consultation through an 'advice file' with the CPS) that cases are 'weak' evidentially; and
- the judgement that there is 'no prospect of a conviction'.

Forty-one complainants were unable to give a clear and coherent account of what happened, but within this group were several women with severe learning difficulties, several with mental health problems, and most were individuals who had been so drunk or drugged that their memory was severely impaired.

In 239 cases the police failed to identify the assailant. From the information provided in the pro formas it appears that DNA tests were conducted in 19 cases, 5 of which resulted in hits on the national database. Although it was stated that there were no forensic findings in 30 cases, it is unclear why DNA testing was not conducted in the remainder of cases. More troubling are the cases (at least 27) where the assailant was not traced – their identity was known, but they were never formally interviewed. In at least eight instances the suspect absconded when first contacted. Several of our interviewees (n=7) were in this group, and were less than impressed by the police investigation.

> [H]e contacted the police, and said oh, it was all a big mistake, and could he come and see them? And instead of saying, "No, we'll come and see you," they said, "Well come up on Monday" ... So what did he do? Sunday, he got his brother to go down to London, to collect his car, and he caught the first train, bus, walked, whatever, boat, out of the country. Gone.
>
> (St Mary's Service User Interview 7, Undetected)

> They haven't even tried, because I have seen him a couple of times since, so there's a general area where he's likely to be, sort of car that he drives, I got the beginning of the registration number, and there's a strong possibility he's a builder, and I saw him come out of a builders' merchants and they haven't followed that up or anything.
>
> (Comparison, Interview 5, Undetected)

For the remaining cases, police decision-making turned on evidential issues connected to the complainant, largely where the victim's account was either regarded with suspicion or not supported by other evidence: in 17 cases the victim's credibility was explicitly referred to; in 10 cases the issue of previous allegations was seen to cast doubt on the current complaint; in 27 inconsistencies or lies were referred to; and in 26 the police and/or CPS took the view that sex was consensual (in 5 of these cases it is suggested that the complainant agreed). In a further seven cases the complainant failed to pick out the suspect in an ID line-up.

The 37 cases designated 'no prospect of conviction' were all submitted to the CPS for advice. In almost all the cases factors related to the complainant were the reason for dropping the case: three had learning difficulties, three had other forms of disability, three had mental health problems and three had made previous allegations (not mutually exclusive). The other cases referred to issues of inconsistency and consent.

The following examples from police pro formas gives a sense of the way decisions regarding cases that are dropped on grounds of insufficient evidence are presented.

Box B: *Examples of insufficient evidence cases from police pro formas*

AP (Aggrieved Party) lied to the police throughout the enquiry and CPS felt there was no evidence. AP lied about drug intake and amount of alcohol consumed. Toxicology tests proved she was extremely drunk and high on cannabis. Advice file submitted to CPS: Issues were lack of victim credibility.   (St Mary's, Pro forma 11)

No forensic evidence, no CCTV evidence, no description of offenders.

(St Mary's, Pro forma 77)

Advice file to CPS regarding incident and discrepancies with AP/offender/witness accounts of what actually happened. CPS advised no charge due to fact that unable to determine whether AP had been raped or gave consent .   (St Mary's, Pro forma 87)

Suffers from learning difficulties ... No offences disclosed. Social Services dealing with persons concerned. 1) AP's tendency to make false allegations. 2) The alleged suspect's inability to have sex due to a medical condition. 3) Lack of forensic, medical or witness corroboration.   (St Mary's, Pro forma 141)

IP (Injured Party) aware – investigation complete. No further action to be taken against alleged offender. This was a case of consensual anal intercourse with consent. Consent which is said to have been obtained through fear of violence.   (REACH, Pro forma 823)

Reason for not proceeding IP found to be unreliable, CPS decision due to previous allegations made by IP.   (REACH, Pro forma 598)

Likely to be undetected. Father has been interviewed, denies offence, leaving one word against other. Anticipated CPS advice NFA due to time lapse between offence and disclosure. Enquiries still ongoing with mental institutions to establish if earlier disclosures. Final outcome: undetected.   (Comparison, Pro forma 1576)

Two previous studies (Harris and Grace, 1999; Lea *et al.*, 2003) document the failure of cases involving women with learning difficulties and mental health problems to progress through the system. This is especially concerning given the accumulation of data that women in these groups are targeted for sexual assault. Whilst the new sexual offences legislation may provide a new route for women with severe learning difficulties[41], this would not affect the majority of cases in this sample. It could be argued that for this group of women the justice gap is a chasm, which will not be bridged unless specific attention is devoted to developing prosecution strategies that provide redress for extremely vulnerable victims.

Another concerning issue is the impact of previous allegations on decision-making, the majority of cases where this issue is mentioned were dropped at an early point (see also Jordan, 2001b). The data on multiple attendees at St Mary's suggest that there is a group of women who are subjected to repeat sexual victimisation by different assailants. Currently, this vulnerability appears to function as a cue to practitioners to dismiss their allegations rather swiftly. Indeed, it could be argued that the entire attrition process results in thousands of people each year entering a group that, should they have the misfortune to be assaulted in the future, will mean their complaint will be treated with even greater scepticism.

One of the most perplexing aspects of police investigation were a number of cases in which 'witnesses' were presented as 'proving' that the sexual encounter had been consensual, or as supporting this interpretation. In no case was there any suggestion that these 'witnesses' were present when sex took place, but their evidence was deemed more credible than the complainant's account (this was also true in a further nine cases with respect to named suspects, who in interview claimed consent). One of the interviewees had this experience and provides insight into the chasm between her account and perception, and how the investigation was conducted.

> I just felt as though they were going through the motions really. The forensic stuff never even got sent off … I was just frustrated – basically the investigation consisted of getting them in and them giving their story, sending off questionnaires to students at the college I was at, because the college didn't want the police to come in because they didn't want them to be a visible presence … And people wrote really helpful comments like, "She appeared to be really happy in their company in the evening," which of course I was, because I hadn't just been assaulted by them at the time! You know, really helpful comments like that which the police sort of put to me afterwards. I thought "Well what the hell relevance is that to what happened afterwards?" … I mean the officer in charge of the case never actually set eyes on me. The impression he gave me over the phone was he didn't believe me from the word go, and I thought, "You've never even met me, you don't know me". I just got the impression he couldn't really be bothered to come over here and meet me because it was a bit of a drive … He basically just said to me, "I've got your file in

---

41. The Sexual Offences Act, 2003, contains a strict liability offence for people deemed to not have the capacity to consent.

front of me, I've taken it to my senior and he says there's not a case, it wouldn't stand up in court." And I asked him to go through what was there: "Well, we've got questionnaires and people said things like the fact that you seemed quite happy chatting to them before". He kept saying, "I'm not saying anything but you know how it could look". I felt he wasn't just saying how it could look, he was saying, "This is how it looks to me" … At the moment I'm just left thinking a terrible thing happened and all I got after it was a load of shit … Nothing is different to how it would have been if I'd not said anything, apart from the fact that I'd still be on the course. And I'd have completed.   (St Mary's, Service User Interview 11, Undetected)

In the research data, little indication was found of early consultations between the police and CPS resulting in further investigation, or that effort was put into building evidence that might support the complainant's account. In the case above, for example, the woman concerned could not understand why the friend she had phoned first and her husband who had been witness to the impacts of the sexual assault on her had not been interviewed, yet a lot of emphasis was placed on questionnaire responses from people who hardly knew her. There were also a number of pro formas where the investigating police officers questioned CPS advice that there was insufficient evidence to charge. During interviews several police officers admitted to being confused as to precisely what CPS needed in order to proceed with a prosecution.

I feel there's different standards within CPS depending on who's assessing the papers … I had a case where … the decision file went into CPS, that came back, discontinued, before even the toxicology reports had come back from the lab. I was really quite disheartened … I feel like whenever you have one that comes down to [an] issue of consent, unless you have areas of bruising, tearing, damage or whatever, from the medical examination as supporting evidence, it is going to be one word against another, and very, very few of those cases ever get to court whereby that IP [Injured Party] is given the opportunity to put his or her side across. I just feel that the CPS give up too easy, too soon.
(REACH, Police Officer CID/Sexual Offence Liaison Officer (SOLO), F1, May 2003)

I don't know how they reach their decisions but I find them on the whole very negative. I think they always want the easy option out so, say you have a victim under the age of sixteen, they are always going 'Oh, we can drop this to a USI[42]' and they never really want to pursue the rape.
(REACH, Police Officer SOLO, F7, May 2003)

---

42. USI – unlawful sexual intercourse.

Practice within CO14 – Clubs and Vice, in the Metropolitan Police – who investigate cases of sexual exploitation, including trafficking, has been to seek early meetings between police, CPS and the prosecuting council. These help to explore where weaknesses in a case might be and what additional evidence might support women involved in prostitution who have reported sexual assault. This echoes the efforts of some Sex Crime Units in the USA, where a commitment to finding ways to prosecute what have previously been deemed 'unprosecutable' cases (Vasschs, 1994), has fundamentally altered the structure and content of investigations. The movement in 2004 to locating CPS lawyers in police stations and for the CPS to take over responsibility for charging, could provide a route to such productive inter-agency work, but only if the investigation and prosecution of rape cases is fundamentally reassessed. Without this the outcome will simply be a faster route to the large number of advice files (n=330 in this sample) returned with a recommendation that 'no further action' is taken.

Whilst there are undoubtedly a proportion of cases in this category that could never be prosecuted effectively, there are equally others where lack of care and commitment in the investigative process along with preconceived stereotypes and attitudes have contributed to the justice gap. Jordan (2001b) reached similar conclusions, based on analysis of police files in New Zealand, noting that police officers (and in the context of this project also prosecutors) used evidential difficulties that might arise as ways of judging genuineness. The veracity of victims/survivors was assessed on the basis of how the practitioners thought both the judge and jury would respond. This creates a discriminatory response to rape compared with other crimes, since it increases the amount of evidence needed to convince a police officer and/or prosecutor that an offence has taken place, and in some cases such judgements are being made before a full investigation has taken place (Jordan, 2001b).

Summary

- Evidential issues account for over one-third of cases lost at the police stage (21% insufficient evidence, 13% offender not identified and 2% no prospect of conviction).
- Within this group there were a number of complainants, often with learning difficulties or mental health issues, who were unable to give the police a clear account of the assault.
- DNA testing appeared to be conducted in a minority of cases.
- There were at least 27 cases where the offender was identified but failed to be traced by the police.
- In a substantial number of cases where the offender was identified the decision not to proceed was linked to victim credibility.

- The pro formas indicated that consultation between police and CPS rarely led to further investigation or enhanced case-building.

Attrition point 4: early withdrawal

A significant group of cases (34%, n=633) lost at an early stage is where victims/survivors opt out of the process at an early stage. In half of these cases (n=315), victims 'declined to complete the initial process'. Below complainants' experiences of the early investigation, including elements of practice or treatment that contributed to some declining to proceed is discussed. In addition, there were 318 cases that constitute early withdrawals (a smaller number – 40 – of late withdrawals are dealt with in subsequent sections), which are also discussed drawing on analysis of the case-tracking database, the police pro formas, questionnaires and interviews with service users, and interviews with police officers and other SARC staff.

Victims who decline to complete the initial process

This group represents some of the very earliest lost cases. According to the police pro formas 315 individuals did this (12% of 2,643 reporting to the police) in relation to one or more of the following: making a formal complaint; forensic examination; giving a statement; or withholding information. However, it is worth noting that this outcome was more common in the areas without an integrated SARC (see Appendix 5). The latter category refers to cases where the complainant refused to name their attacker (or more rarely where the assault took place), and whilst in some cases it was clear that they knew the person well, in others it was unclear whether they could have identified either the assailant or the location of the assault. Another group includes those who fail to respond to police efforts to contact them, or who move without leaving a forwarding address.

The contribution of SARCs to responses to reported rape is addressed in another publication, as are the varying processes involved in reporting at the six research sites (see Lovett et al., 2004). Prior to a forensic examination, however, complainants will have had contact with at least two police officers: one to whom they make the first report, and one who makes arrangements for the examination and accompanies them. This officer is likely to take basic details of the offence, so that preliminary phases of the investigation with respect to the crime scene and suspect can begin, although in some instances a full statement appears to be taken before the forensic examination.[43]

---

43. Internationally there is now increasing recognition that a fuller and more accurate statement is likely if it is taken a day or two after the initial report (see, Jordan, 2001b).

Here findings that, from the perspective of complainants, illustrate points where either service provision or the behaviour of personnel do or do not create a context of support and confidence in the process are focused on. Responses to the service user questionnaires illustrate that the availability of women – police officers, crisis workers and forensic examiners – was important for the majority (52%, n=93 for the initial police response; 65%, n=85 for the statement; and 83%, n=90 for the forensic examination). Whilst one of the interviewees and Jordan's (2002) research make it clear that this is not a case of 'any woman will do', the vehemence with which almost half of the questionnaire respondents articulated their feelings suggests that the absence of a female doctor may result in some complainants refusing a forensic examination, and the lack of a trained female police officer may at worst mean they do not make a statement, or at best provide a less detailed one. Reasons for preferring female police officers were expressed either in terms of not being able to talk to or trust a man (33%, n=44) or it being easier to talk to a female (26%, n=35), reflecting findings of previous studies (see, for example, Jordan, 2001a and Temkin, 1999).

If possible just female officers. I knew I was safe with the male officers, I just couldn't cope at the time. (St Mary's, Q1, 1051)

It was extremely difficult telling [a] female what had happened – I couldn't have done it if it was a male. (REACH, Q1, 3003)

I had just been raped by a male, I didn't want to have a male to talk to at that time. (STAR, Q1, 2082)

I felt embarrassed, awkward, didn't want to tell him the intimate details. (Comparison, Q1, 4005)

Every woman/man who has been assaulted, please give them female officers, or at least a choice. (St Mary's, Q1, 1008)

Although over two-thirds (70%, n=121) of questionnaire respondents evaluated the initial police response positively, a significant minority (30%, n=53) did not. Interestingly, this varied across the four sites with the highest levels of dissatisfaction registered in the STAR area (46%, n=28).

Preferences for female practitioners were even more pronounced with respect to the forensic examination (see Lovett *et al.*, 2004 for more details), and both were echoed in interviews.

A lady came down from the local police station, really nice woman. And just took some sort of basic details at first, you know, related to the assault, and that was fine ... (a) I was glad it was a woman, (b) she believed me ... that was my first contact with the police, so that was really important and that was good. And she didn't want to know too much at that stage ... Everybody at this stage believed me, my friends, my husband, the doctor, the policewoman.

(St Mary's, Service User Interview 11, Undetected)

They gave me the option of whether I wanted a female or a male doctor as well ... [and that was important] 'cause it's not really very comfortable at the best of times having them kind of things done, and I imagine it's worse at the best of times with a male than with a female, but at the worst of times, it's a lot better having a female!

(STAR, Service User Interview 15, Undetected)

The forensic examination itself was experienced, almost universally, as a difficult and intrusive process, made more problematic when one or more of the following factors applied: lack of a female examiner; delay in arranging an examination; unpleasant environment; and the manner of individual professionals. A small percentage of police referrals to the SARCs declined to have the forensic examination (2%, n=40).

It could be speculated that this group contains those who are most ambivalent about the reporting process, since they take their decisions at the earliest point possible. However, responses from the questionnaires suggest that additional factors are at play. Sixteen of the 188 respondents who reported had chosen not to make a formal statement, and police attitudes – either being disbelieved or discouraged from proceeding – and the CJS process more generally were uppermost for over half (five of eight) of those who provided an explanation.

The police officers at the station after saying it wouldn't be in the public interest to get it into court.   (St Mary's, Q1, 1023)

The CID were blunt and unsympathetic. They said if I made a formal complaint they would have to question the neighbours – but I wanted to keep it quiet out of embarrassment.   (St Mary's, Q1, 1060)

Police said he had witnesses, so I felt as if they didn't believe me. (STAR, Q1, 2002)

The DC didn't believe me, called me a liar.   (STAR, Q1, 2080)

*[I] was told [by police] because of history [of drug abuse] it could not go further but
[I] could make a statement if [I] still wanted.* (Comparison 1, Q1, 4015)

That the behaviour of police officers plays a part in the earliest withdrawals is further supported by the fact that more declined to give a statement or make a formal complaint than refused the forensic medical, an inherently difficult and intrusive procedure (Kelly, 2003a). In the context of uncertainty and trauma, professionals need to be skilled in order to build rapport and trust, and police officers have a responsibility to conduct a thorough investigation. In some of these instances neither appeared to be the case.

The process of statement-taking was also inconsistent, with almost three-quarters of questionnaire respondents (73%, n=114 of 156 where times known) making a statement immediately or on the day after reporting, 15 per cent (n=24) up to one week later and 12 per cent (n=18) over a week after reporting. Just under one-quarter (23%, n=35) said they had been under pressure to provide an immediate statement. Experiences of making a statement among the interviewees revealed that 20 of the 43 who made one described the process favourably, but 20 described it negatively, while the remaining three did not express an opinion. Being too tired and confused to provide an accurate account, feeling judged or disbelieved, insensitive questioning, the length of time taken due to statements having to be hand-written and not being able to recall details were the predominant issues. The latter applied particularly to interviewees who suspected drugs had been used in their assaults, or who had been assaulted when they were drunk.

It is a concern that over a tenth of complainants in the case-tracking sample chose not to complete the first stages of an investigation is concerning. A number of cases, however, revealed that the complexity of individual circumstances and potential consequences of an investigation could be the deciding factor. For example: the report was made by a health professional following disclosure to them, but against the wishes of the victim/survivor; the report was made by someone else and the victim/survivor was ambivalent; details of the rape emerged in an investigation of domestic violence (in half this was post-separation), in which the woman was seeking protection and never considered pursuing a rape charge[44]; finding the prospect of an investigation where one's family, friends and/or work colleagues will not only find out, but also be questioned, too hard to bear; and finally wanting to forget/deal with the assault in one's own way. That some people decide a rape investigation is either not what they sought, or not what they can sustain, is likely to remain the case however much the services and responses of professionals become more attuned to the realities of rape and sexual assault.

---

44. In several of these the police officer noted that woman made explicit comments about not wanting to pursue a rape complaint for the sake of her children.

Provision of female examiners and trained female police officers at the initial stages is clearly important for many complainants (including the majority of male respondents), and essential for a small proportion. Questionnaire and interview data also make clear that a climate of belief, privacy, feeling safe and reassured by the professionalism of staff creates a context in which difficult processes can be endured. Equally the absence of these elements can contribute to a context in which confidence is eroded at the outset, which can either become a factor in withdrawal or affect the quality and content of evidence-gathering.

Early victim withdrawals

An additional group (n=318), whilst completing the initial processes of a forensic examination and formal statement, withdrew during the early investigative stage. Cross-tabulations using the case-tracking database, comparing this group with cases that proceeded (n=527), revealed the following.

- Complainants aged 16 to 35 accounted for a greater proportion of the withdrawal group (72%, n=228) compared with the proceeding group (63%, n=332), whilst for under-16s the opposite was the case (9%, n=29 withdrawn compared with 20%, n=103 proceeding). The age group most associated with withdrawal were 16- to 25-year-olds, who constituted almost half of all those who withdrew (48%, n=153 compared with 42%, n=221 in the proceeding group).
- Those currently in a relationship – either married or living together – were slightly more likely to withdraw (53%, n=63 compared with 47%, n=55 where case proceeding).
- In terms of the relationship with the perpetrator, the only cases that showed any distinct variation were those involving current partners, which represented a slightly higher proportion of those in the withdrawal group than the proceeding group (17%, n=48 versus 10%, n=52). In contrast, the proportion of those involving family members in the proceeding group was twice that of those in the withdrawal group (9%, n=45 versus 4%, n=11). Of all cases involving known perpetrators twice as many appeared to be proceeding than being withdrawn (65%, n=350 compared with 35%, n=185).
- The involvement of drugs or alcohol appeared to have some impact on rates of withdrawal. Cases involving both were more likely to be withdrawn (57%, n=31 compared with 43%, n=23). When taken individually, though, this was more marked in relation to drugs (54%, n=43 withdrawn versus 46%, n=37 proceeding) than alcohol (44%, n=127 withdrawn versus 56%, n=159 proceeding).

In only one-fifth (21%, n=66) of cases did the police pro formas provide any details on the reasons for victim withdrawals, although it is notable that, compared to no crimes and insufficient evidence, there were far fewer references to either victim characteristics or evidential problems here. Where there is information, for half of the complainants (n=33) fear of the court process was the deciding factor, 15 refer to complainants' uncertainty about whether they were raped, including some thinking it may have been consensual, seven state that the person 'wants to put the event behind them', and another seven complainants are reported to have made the decision after consultation with their family. From the police information, in at least 13 of these cases the assailant was a current/ex-partner, which may have played a part in the decision (in six cases it clearly did).

There are 74 cases in which the complainant withdrew where the offender had not yet been identified, which accounted for just under one-quarter (23%) of all victim withdrawals. Since there is no immediate prospect of a court case, this decision represents, on some level, a loss of faith in the CJS – either in the ability of the police to detect the offender, or in the process at a more interactional level with individual officers. The woman speaking below also illustrates that perceived slackness and failure to maintain contact can prompt withdrawal, prevented in this instance by St Mary's facilitating discussion.

They didn't phone me. I phoned them in July to find out what was happening, 'cause it was just screwing me up, 'cause I didn't know where he was and I was having panic attacks, looking round me all the time whenever I went anywhere ... I felt the police were totally unsupportive and they didn't understand how I felt ... I came here [St Mary's] with the decision that I was dropping the case. X then contacted [police station], and spoke to them, and then it was decided that I was to talk to the police again. And lo and behold, two weeks later, I'm sat in here again, with the police telling me all this information about this guy that they might have told me beforehand. Like the fact that he's got a history ... he was accused of sexually harassing two members of staff. And then he was accused after he'd left of actually sexually abusing a patient. And at that point I thought, "Well I can understand why the police are so keen to get him" – I was what we call a "date rape", next time it might be somebody off the street. So I said, "OK, fine, go ahead, yes, I'm prepared to carry on with this." And since then, bugger all. Nothing. And I phoned them the other week to tell them I've moved house: "Right, OK, fine, goodbye" ... Hey, you know, I'm a victim here, and I get absolutely nothing, nothing from the police, at all ... I just feel that the police, after the initial excitement, it's almost as if you're forgotten. You're a forgotten statistic, and that doesn't help. I'm surprised more people don't drop out. And if they do, that would be why. Because the police don't maintain contact with you. (St Mary's Service User Interview 7, Undetected)

There are also nine unusual cases, five where the suspects admitted the crimes (one handed himself in to the police station) and four where a stranger rapist was identified from the DNA database. All would have been strong evidentially, but the complainants still withdrew. Again one has to ask whether in the interim period they had lost confidence in the CJS.

Another pattern involved suspect interviews (n=42) and/or arrests (n=30); in at least one-third the offence was either denied or sex was claimed to be consensual. Withdrawal seemed to follow this fairly closely, possibly when police returned to put these versions of events to the complainant.

Just under half (45%, n=74) of questionnaire respondents who reported had either withdrawn their complaint or were unsure about pursuing a legal case at this stage. Their comments further illustrate that fear of court process, and especially anticipation of having to give public testimony about intimate intrusions, having one's behaviour scrutinised and judged and the prospect of acquittal were powerful disincentives.

Reliving it, being questioned in court. Too upsetting to go to court.
(St Mary's, Q1, 1037)

Why put myself through all that to have a court say that it's not worth it.
(St Mary's, Q1, 1023)

I couldn't bear the cross-examination or being made to feel in the wrong.
(REACH, Q1, 3026)

Giving evidence in front of strangers. I wouldn't stand a chance in court.
(REACH, Q1, 3047)

Scared I won't be believed, but I feel guilty 'cause he may hurt others.
(STAR, Q1, 2040)

Because I feel I will not be believed due it being from a partner continuing over several years.
(STAR, Q1, 2052)

There were also several examples of witness intimidation, which had clearly not been addressed or stopped.

I never took him to court, due to the harassment I have been getting from this person and his friends.
(St Mary's, Q2, 1023)

For a significant group, thinking beyond reporting to the potential of appearing in court is a major barrier to continued engagement with the CJS. There were also a small number of cases where the police officer provided enough detail to make clear that they had doubts about the account provided by the complainant, which they put to them forcibly – it was following this that the withdrawal took place. The authors' data from complainants themselves underline that the tone, content and timing of providing information about the low conviction rate can act as a prompt to withdrawal.

> I think they should give the benefit of the doubt more ... They were acting like they were there that night and they knew what had already happened ... it felt like "we've done all this before, we know what's going to come out of it" ... they were giving all this negative stroking, not one positive to anything ... Everything I said they questioned back at me. "Why did you go there?", and then I'd tell them why "Well he said this or he said that." Like everything I did they had a question to come back at me ... It felt like he was the victim and I'd done something wrong ... I'm not a police officer so I don't know, but the questioning I thought were disgusting, the way they treated me. I thought, "If anybody else has been through what I've been through no wonder they don't press charges" ... Before I went in the interview room she was dead nice and dead posh, but as soon as I got in that room she just went dead stern: "This is what it will be like in court. This is all the questions, you're going to have, tough questions" ... If it ever happened again – I hope it never does – I don't think I'd even bother going to the police. There's no point ... They were just like talking me out of it ... That negatively influenced me, definitely ... I'm not so much angry at him, I'm angry at the police. They're supposed to be a public service, and they failed me.
>
> (St Mary's, Service User Interview 4, Detected no proceedings)

> This officer was like "I just don't believe you." And, I mean, I could have swung for her because she said to me "Oh well I'm trained in this," I'm thinking, "You're not," because from the moment I saw her, it's like "You're trying it on." "You are just making this up" ... It was her body language and certain things she said ... I wasn't interested to take it any further.
>
> (REACH, Service User Interview 6, Status unknown)

Over one-third (n=26) of the police officers interviewed across all the research sites concurred that the fear of court is one of the main reasons why complainants withdraw from the process.

There may be a perception about getting into court and having to relive it all. Having everything be brought up and dragged up again and their whole life and lifestyle examined in a courtroom. That can put somebody off completely. Some people just can't face the ordeal, and it is an ordeal going to court.

(St Mary's, Police Officer DC, M9, March 2003)

I think some people just genuinely don't want to face the court system, which is understandable because it's still quite an adversarial thing for them to go through, it's not a pleasant experience, and I think people think that – certainly rape victims think – they may be questioned about their sexual history. I think that does put a lot of people off. Once they've sat down and thought about it.

(STAR, Police Officer CID, M8, April 2003)

The court case, they know that court cases are and can be traumatic, and that your character can be called into question and you can be cross-examined over a long period. I think that definitely puts people off. I suppose their whole sexual life is aired in public, basically.   (Comparison 1, Police Officer DC, M1, June 2002)

Fear of going to court was also cited by the majority of SARC staff and key informants as the most significant factor in withdrawal from the criminal justice process. Their responses were typified by the following comment.

Some of them feel that they'll be torn to pieces.

(STAR, Case Tracker, F1, December 2001)

The interviews with police officers revealed very little consistency in both when complainants were given details on the process and the type of information provided. Over half of those who had early contact with complainants were clear that they gave this information at the earliest possible point, and many thought that being 'realistic' was in the complainant's best interests. These are examples of the 'second guessing' that other researchers have identified in CJS responses to rape (see Kersetter, 1990 with respect to the police and Frohmann, 1991 with respect to prosecutors), with each tier basing their decisions on the responses they expect or predict from the next.

I must admit that one of the things that I do, and it's perhaps a wrong thing, but I think you've got to empower the victim. She's got to be the one that's got to make this choice and got to know what she's up against ... then it's her decision. When I talk about what the police can do, one of the things that I do is go into details about what court can mean, the things that can happen. I'm not painting a black picture, I'm painting a truthful picture, so that at no point along the line when they've been in court for three days they can say "You never told me about this."

(St Mary's, Police Officer DC, F10, March 2003)

When someone comes into the police station we are very victim-focused, but we also have to make people aware that in the courts it's a little bit different and they may get a harsher time. We're just being completely honest with these people.

(Comparison 2, Police Officer DS, M1, February 2003)

Nonetheless, a staff member at one of the SARCs identified this as a potential disincentive to proceeding.

Some of the police ... will immediately say to this woman "Do you realise how bad it's going to be in court?" I feel that's far too soon to be making a comment and I think they shouldn't say that. It's almost trying to put her off. It's like I've just been raped and I'm trying to deal with this and now you're telling me, "Do you realise when you go to court they may bring up this, they may bring up that?" ... It's almost like they're testing her out, is she going to go ahead with this, is this real, and I really think this shouldn't be done. A woman's not in a place to be thinking about court within hours or days of being raped. I think that if the police stopped doing that maybe she would actually continue. (REACH, Counsellor, F3, January 2002)

Reflections

Early withdrawals, therefore, fall into several categories: decisions made very quickly which reflect an original doubt/ambivalence about the process which is not allayed (or is possibly even reinforced) by the reporting and early investigative process; those which follow aggressive questioning or discouragement by the police; those where the complainant feels there is nothing to support her account/where the suspect makes clear he will plead consent; and those where the prospect of a trial is too terrifying to contemplate.

Whilst there are many reasons why complainants would be ambivalent about being involved in a rape prosecution, those who have made an official report to the police have, at least in part, expressed an interest in achieving justice. That so many lose confidence so quickly, clearly not believing that the CJS is capable of either recognising their needs and concerns or delivering justice, is surely an indication that there are serious gaps in how reported rape and sexual assault is currently responded to. In this context it is worth reflecting on what lies behind the word 'withdrawal': for victims/survivors this constitutes a withdrawal of trust and confidence, whereas at the official level it is regarded as the withdrawal of the original complaint.

Summary

- Victims who declined to complete the initial process and early victim withdrawals accounted for the largest proportion (34%) of cases lost at the police stage.
- More victims declined to complete the initial process in the areas without an integrated SARC.
- The availability of women police officers, crisis workers and forensic examiners was important for the majority of respondents and interviewees.
- Seventy per cent of respondents were satisfied with the initial police response.
- Twelve per cent of all those who reported declined to complete the initial process by not either making a formal complaint, not having a forensic examination, not giving a statement or withholding information.
- Those respondents who did not make a formal statement cited being disbelieved or discouraged from proceeding by the police and fear of the CJS process as key factors.
- A proportion chose not to proceed as a way of taking back control and/or for other personal reasons.
- The age group most associated with early victim withdrawal were 16- to 25-year-olds.
- Only a small number of police pro formas contained details of the reason for the withdrawal, but where details were known over half cited fear of the court process.
- No offender was identified in just under one-quarter of all withdrawals, suggesting that for these complainants there was a loss of faith in the ability of the police to catch the offender, or in the CJS more broadly.
- Just under half of first questionnaire respondents who reported to the police had withdrawn their complaint or were unsure about pursuing a legal case, and cited fear of court process, the prospect of giving public testimony and being judged as disincentives.
- More than one-third of police officers interviewed agreed that fear of court is one of the main reasons why complainants withdraw from the process.

Attrition point 5 – CPS decision making

Only 527 of the original 2,643 cases were referred through to the CPS for prosecution, meaning that over three-quarters of cases (80%, n=2,116) were lost or dropped at the police stage. Of the 527 just under two-thirds (61%, n=322) proceeded to the trial stage, although in 60 cases the final CPS decision is not known. From the data in Table 4.2, it appears that discontinuance by the CPS is a relatively small element in attrition of cases that reach the CPS (26%, n=38). However, the missing data for this stage and the involvement of the CPS in a significant number of cases where police took decisions after submitting advice files, mean that these data substantially underestimate the CPS role in attrition.

Late victim withdrawals also feature here, with 40 taking place at these stages in the process. Four of our questionnaire respondents were in this group. In one case, the police had advised that the CPS were unlikely to pursue the case, and the complainant also referred to unhelpful preparation for court. The remaining three all referred to fear of court, and one also mentioned her relationship to the offender. That these perceptions were, at least in some cases, linked to information from the police is illustrated by this comment.

> I dropped it because I was too scared and the police said it was a hard case. Not
> many women win the case.   (St Mary's, Q3, 1025)

CPS advice and decisions are taken on the basis of the Code of Practice, which contains a two-level test: an evidential test and one with respect to public interest. Only cases where the evidential test suggests a realistic prospect of conviction are taken forward, and there may be some circumstances where the public interest test is seen as applying in rape cases, most commonly where the vulnerability of the complainant leads to a conclusion that a legal case risks further harm to them.

One issue worth noting here, which might affect decisions on the evidential test, were findings from the analysis of forensic medical reports and police statements. In a minority of cases, information which was not relevant to the case was recorded, which could provide a 'back door' route to the introduction of sexual history evidence. In a small number of medical reports references were found to prostitution, contraception and previous abuse. Fifty police statements (31 St Mary's, 19 STAR) were analysed. Seven of these statements contained irrelevant material, which in four cases (all from the St Mary's area) related to previous sexual history, and was particularly notable in a case involving a gay man, where extensive details of his sexual life were recorded. This was further confirmed by questionnaire respondents: over half (58%, n=93 of 160 who made formal statements) had been asked about their sexual history. Within this group, one-third (33%, n=30) were asked about their prior or current relationship with the alleged assailant, 19 per cent (n=17) about their sex life generally and 48 per cent (n=44) were asked about both these issues. Whilst a current relationship with a suspect is relevant to the facts of a case, anything beyond this recorded in a statement may enable the protections of section 41 of the Youth Justice and Criminal Evidence Act, which limits contexts where sexual history evidence can be introduced in court, to be evaded (Temkin, 2003). Concerns about credibility of the victim/witness play a part in assessments at the CPS stage (HMCPSI, 2002), and it will be especially concerning if irrelevant discrediting material is present in disclosable evidence.

There is a discernable shift within the CPS from independence and separation from other agencies, and a particular interpretation of 'objectivity', to engagement with inter-agency processes and recognising the needs of victims of crime. In relation to rape, there is also a policy change with respect to the development of specialisation. These changes are, however, very new and their implementation inconsistent. Whilst these moves are welcome, they need to be linked to a focus on building cases. One recent development worth noting here is the practice in Newcastle CPS of attempting to learn through formal reports from counsel from both successful and unsuccessful prosecutions, especially acquittals, in order to feed back into better case preparation.

Summary

- Only a small proportion of reported cases were discontinued at the CPS stage. However, this underestimates CPS' role, since they offer opinions on large numbers of advice files.
- A small number of forensic medical reports and police statements contained inappropriate material on complainants' previous sexual history that may have affected CPS assessments of their credibility.
- The CPS needs to build on recent moves towards specialisation and place greater emphasis on building cases.

Attrition point 6 – court and trial

Of the 2,643 reports, 322 (12%) were scheduled for trial. This is equivalent to 14 per cent of all 2,244 reported cases where the outcome is known. Eleven per cent (n=34) failed to reach this point due to either late withdrawal, the CPS deciding not to offer evidence or judge-ordered acquittals. This outcome was most likely for cases involving 16- to 25-years-olds (n=15), and over two-thirds of these cases involved known offenders (n=23). Around half of all convictions were due to guilty pleas (49%, n=89 of 183) rather than findings by a jury. Table 4.2 highlighted that, where a full trial took place (n=181)[45], an acquittal was more likely to be the outcome than a conviction (57%, n=104 acquittals compared with 43%, n=77 part or full convictions).

Factors associated with conviction

Cases (n=183) that resulted in a finding of guilt (guilty pleas and whole or part convictions at trial) have been compared with all other reported cases in the sample (n=2,460), on a range of factors. Those factors associated with conviction are listed below.

- Cases involving under-16s were more likely to result in a finding of guilt (15%, n=55), a rate more than twice as high as for those aged 26 to 35 (6%, n=36) and almost four times higher than for those aged 16 to 25 (4%, n=52).
- Age is an even more pronounced factor where trial outcomes are considered. Trials involving under-16s had an acquittal rate of 20 per cent (n=14), whereas for those involving adults this was twice as high at 41 per cent (n=90). The group most associated with acquittal was 16- to 25-year-olds, among whom the acquittal rate was 51 per cent (n=54).
- Cases involving at least one known offender were slightly more likely to result in conviction (9%, n=117), followed by strangers (5%, n=40), whilst recent acquaintances had the lowest rate (4%, n=13). However, these findings need to be contextualised in a number of ways: cases involving known offenders always involved a named offender, whereas for those involving strangers the offender was identified in only a minority of cases; in one-third (32%, n=37) of the known offender convictions the complainant was under16.
- The absence of alcohol or drugs was associated with conviction, and was slightly more likely in the case of alcohol (8%, n=70 versus 5%, n=42) but over three times more with respect to drugs (7%, n=107 versus 2%, n=6).
- Whilst injury alone had little impact, cases involving the use of a weapon and resulting external injuries were twice as likely to result in conviction compared with those where neither was present (7%, n=12 versus 3%, n=81).
- Convictions were obtained in four per cent (n=7) of reported cases involving women with disabilities and in 11 per cent (n=7) of those involving women in prostitution.

---

45. Includes acquittals and part and full convictions, but excludes the 17 cases where the outcome of guilty plea or conviction was unclear.

- Only three per cent (n=8) of reported cases involving multiple perpetrators resulted in convictions. Seven of these cases involved two perpetrators and one involved three.

These data suggest that whilst some aspects of rape cases mean they are more likely to result in convictions, it is not impossible to prosecute successfully where they are absent. Nonetheless, the 'real rape' template features strongly, and our data suggest that the group least likely to find their cases proceeding are those in the 16- to 25-year-old age group.

In terms of the research participants, 20 questionnaire respondents had been to trial, and in another a guilty plea had been offered at the Plea and Directions Hearing; a further nine were awaiting the trial. Outcomes for the 21 respondents were 11 guilty pleas, 4 findings of guilt by the jury and 6 acquittals. In the interview sample 15 cases proceeded to trial, with 6 guilty pleas, 3 findings of guilt at trial and 6 acquittals.

The experience of the lead up to, and actual, trial were draining and disquieting for all research participants.

> I wasn't sleeping, not eating ... I didn't realise you could exist on such a lack of sleep. Because I was going through it all in my head. What if he says this? It was bringing all the feelings I didn't want to feel back ... I knew it would be like being raped all over again. But there would be an audience listening this time. 'Cause of all the people in the court. The jury, and the people that sit there just to listen, all the clerks and the barrister, the judge, the one – the usher that takes the oath – they're like the audience, aren't they? The first rape was just between me and 'it'. The second rape is in front of a lot of people. All listening. And you're stood there. And you're trying to explain to these people all the pain and suffering and degradation and violation and how can they possibly comprehend? Because they won't have experienced it. Could I be convincing enough by telling the truth, that they would believe me, or would he con them like he conned me?
>
> (St Mary's, Service User Interview 10, Acquittal)

> I do think that there should be something whereby these kinds of cases are seen within six months. They shouldn't be allowed to drag on. They really shouldn't. It's emotionally wearing on anybody. But to actually drag on for over twelve months, it really is soul-destroying ... Because you just can't get on with your life. You cannot do anything.
>
> (St Mary's, Service User Interview 1, Acquittal)

I think 'cause he was in the courtroom, I think having to see him. And also what were they going to ask me, I don't know, 'cause you just read about ... previous sexual history and they kind of try and make you look bad. I was concerned about that, really, like what I was going to be asked.

(STAR, Service User Interview 14, Conviction)

Well, they made me out to be obviously the town tart, which I wasn't, and they had nothing to prove it, and once in my life I had to have an abortion and they made out that I was such a bad person to have that ... I don't know how they found that [out], and then they tried to make out that I'd had lots of abortions, which was rubbish ... I think it is really hard, because they keep saying in your face "You're lying, you're lying, you're making it up," and you just have to keep saying "I'm not lying," and you just have to stick to it ... but I'm glad I did now because I got to see him give evidence, the lies that he was coming out with, so I could go to my barrister and say "He's lying about this, and I know he's lying about this because I've got proof."

(Comparison, Interview 2, Conviction)

One SARC counsellor highlighted the extent of complainants' fear of what court proceedings might entail.

[They are] absolutely terrified of going to court, and what they always say is, "His defence is going to tear me apart, how am I going to deal with that?" Terrified. Terrified of the brief, terrified of the culture of gowns and wigs and the judge, terrified of being able to see the offender, but most of all what they seem terrified of is bringing up all their past history and him getting off.

(St Mary's, Counsellor, F1, January 2001)

Guilty pleas are undoubtedly the outcome of careful investigation and case preparation, resulting in strong evidence against the accused.[46] Often they are the outcome of plea negotiations, where prosecutors are faced with having a finding of guilt for an offence versus taking the case through the lottery of a criminal trial. At least 30 of the 89 guilty pleas in this sample were to lower charges; 17 involved under-16s, of which 11 were pleas to Unlawful Sexual Intercourse (USI) and four to indecent assault. A guilty plea frequently results in a sentence discount, in part recognising that this saved the victim/witness from having to give evidence. In one case the plea was entered five minutes before the complainant was due to give evidence and she expressed strong reservations about what happened next.

46. In a very few cases there was also some suggestion of a 'guilty conscience' on the part of the perpetrator, in two instances to the extent of giving themselves up to the police at an early stage. These were invariably cases where the rapist was known.

The judge praised him. I was angry. He only did it because all my witnesses turned up. Men who leave the victim till the last minute before going into court should not be congratulated. "Even at the last minute he saved the victim," said the judge. No, he saved himself. They played down the violence, the violence was worse than the rape.

(St Mary's, Q3, 1010)

Better case preparation, and ensuring that no disclosable evidence contains unnecessary material that can be used against the credit of the complainant are undoubtedly factors that increase guilty pleas, and there may well be important lessons to be learnt from cases with this outcome.

The issue of lack of contact between the prosecution – both CPS and the prosecution barrister – was a source of frustration and confusion to many of those whose cases reached court. Five respondents whose cases resulted in acquittals attributed this to the prosecution counsel being poorly prepared, and appearing unfamiliar with the facts of the case.

I know they can't tell me exactly what questions are going to be asked, but I do think it unfair that I can't even meet the person who is going to represent me. Even if just to give a personal impression, even if it was just a 20 minute chat … I just feel it's so unjust when he has had twelve months of support and legal assistance. It's his word against mine, and he's had twelve months to get his speech rehearsed, whereas I haven't … I found it terrible, I really did, I thought I'm just as entitled to speak to somebody. They said, "You'll get to see the statement before you go in." I just thought – so that's it! The statement was made in a state of shock, for one thing, and I do know there's things I haven't said that probably I should have … My version of events didn't come out at all. He didn't ask anything. He [prosecution barrister] just made a statement. "Oh you went this way, and you had a drink here", and I said, "Yes." "And he attacked you on this particular spot," and I'm thinking "Well, surely I've got to give more than this" … He didn't ask questions, he was reading from a piece of paper all the time. And I thought, "He's not even read the evidence, he's not seen it at all" … I'm stood there thinking, "You should be saying something, and he didn't say a thing … He should have intervened more … I think if I'd just been able to stand there and say what was on my statement, my version of events, things would've been so different … After [giving evidence] I said, "I can't believe it, this is going to go against me, I know it is. At one stage he didn't even know my name." And the police said, "Oh, he's really quite good." That was on the Monday. And I found out on the Thursday that he'd got away with it. (St Mary's, Service User Interview 1, Acquittal)

Two main witness statements weren't at court, vital information details weren't brought to the court. Why is it [that] the defendant has a solicitor on hand able to see all that is being brought to the trial yet the victim has nothing?

(STAR, Q2, 2092)

I had no idea what I was going to be asked by my barrister, and I remember his first opening question and I'd never been asked this, either, nobody had said to me, you know, "What was your first sexual experience?" or, you know, "Have you had sex before?" And, funnily enough, it wasn't actually my boyfriend at the time that I'd first slept with, so the barrister asked the question, and inevitably the answer came out, "Oh, it was a friend of mine," you know, which obviously starts off the wrong impression in the minds of the jury, and it sort of went downhill from there, really... I mean, looking back now, he was obviously trying to paint a picture of somebody who, you know, had a sort of impeccable sexual history and that had only ever slept with one person and was in a relationship etc., I had never been told about that, they didn't know that I'd already slept with somebody else. The look on the barrister's face when I answered was absolute horror. And, yeah, they'd never asked the question. Unfortunately for me ... and yet I never met the solicitor preparing the case.

(STAR, Service User Interview 20, Acquittal)

It was not part of this project to observe rape trials, but all studies of adversarial systems report that cross-examination is uniformly described by complainants as savage and gruelling (see, for example, Department of Women, 1996; Lees, 2002), focusing on whatever aspect might undermine the credibility of the complainant. The extent to which defence barristers are prepared to deploy outmoded gender stereotypes and legacies of victim/woman blame has also been documented (Temkin, 2000b). Within this, the spectre of 'real rape' recurs and is reproduced. These factors play a part in the acquittal rate of more than 50 per cent in rape trials.

Reflections

Two American law professors (Schulhofer, 1998; Taslitz, 1999) conclude that how rape narratives are, and are not, constructed as 'believable' in the courtroom has more influence than statute changes and even evidential requirements. Moreover, it is the failure to address this that accounts for the failure of legal reform.

The inability to engage with cultural narratives and macho adversarialism explains rape law reform's failure. These primary mechanisms by which rape jurors determine credibility are unchanged. Consequently, unjustified acquittals mount.

(Taslitz, 1999, pp154-5)

The most powerful and persistent cultural narratives are the notion of 'real rape' and that women frequently lie about rape.

Such a perception outweighs, in many cases, evidence of resistance and visible injuries sustained by the victim, or even gross inconsistencies, changed stories and 'lies' in the defendant's account. (Jordan, 2001b, p72)

Summary

- Twelve per cent of all reported cases, or 14 per cent of those where the outcome is known, reached the trial stage.
- A proportion of these did not proceed to trial due to late withdrawal or the case being discontinued at court.
- Around half of all convictions were due to guilty pleas rather than verdicts.
- In cases where a full trial took place an acquittal was more likely to be the outcome than a conviction and the acquittal rate in trials involving adults was twice as high as in those involving under-16s.

5.   Challenges, dilemmas and recommendations

The combined analysis of the St Mary's database and the prospective attrition research provide a more detailed picture of the processes underlying attrition than has previously been possible. Some of the findings support the claim of police officers that they are faced with a complex mix of cases, some of which are false allegations and some of which do not involve a sexual offence. Even within these categories, however, one cannot take all police designations at face value, since a proportion are contested by some complainants, and regarded with scepticism by researchers. It is, however, clear that around six per cent (n=160)[47] of initial reports are either false complaints or cases where early investigation reveals no evidence of an assault. These are cases where 'no crime' has taken place, and the data suggest that the majority of such cases were identified at an early point.

There is also a proportion of cases where contact with the CJS is tentative, or not chosen by the complainant themselves. The St Mary's police liaison officer reflected on these complexities early in the project.

> When people ring the police or involve the police, it's at that critical moment, when something has happened or is happening and they want help. I'm not always convinced that the help they want is a rape investigation. The help they want might be "Just get me out of this situation, you know, get me home, get me safe", and that's why they ring the police. Very often people haven't fully thought through the consequences of what ringing the police actually means. And so perhaps what does happen is that people want a service at that time, and that then gets them into the sausage machine of the investigation and perhaps they never wanted to be in that sausage machine anyway. And it's very difficult to get out of it, other than at some point saying "Well, look, hang on, I'm withdrawing from this."
>
> (St Mary's, Police Liaison, January 2001)

Whilst acknowledging that this may well be the case for some, this study's data suggest that the ambivalence many complainants feel relates to the processes of investigation and prosecution: the practical challenges of a forensic examination; making a statement; the prospect of courtroom testimony; and their experience and perception of treatment at each stage by the professionals involved. Decisions to report and to continue with the case are

---

47. Included here are all no evidence of assault cases (n=83), and those false allegations deemed probable and possible (n=77).

made when an interest in justice and protection for themselves and others outweighs the potential costs, and where victims/survivors feel supported in this decision. This is a fine balance, which CJS professionals and support services, through their actions and inactions, can tip one way or the other.

The belief amongst some CJS professionals that many complaints are false, that victims are to blame for 'risk-taking', places unreasonable requirements on complainants to demonstrate that that they are 'real' and deserving victims. Aware of these implicit standards, many victims/survivors adjust their initial account in order to appear believable (see also, Jordan, 2001b). The danger is that these omissions and/or evasions are understood through the lens of a false complaint at worst, and as creating evidential problems at best. Both respondents and interviewees stressed the importance of encountering a climate of belief at the initial stages, which enabled them to be more relaxed, and in turn created a space in which trust could develop. In such a context police officers would be in a stronger position to encourage honesty, whilst acknowledging that there may be aspects of what took place which victims/survivors feel uneasy about disclosing. There were a few examples of this occurring in the study sample, including one case where the complainant was involved in prostitution and had a drugs problem. The initial response of the police officers to this information was respectful and open – making clear that they had to tell the CPS, but did not think either fact was relevant to the context of her assault. This case resulted in a guilty plea.

Part of the attrition process is a feedback loop where, given that 80 per cent of cases drop out or are lost in the earliest stages (see Table 4.2), everyone – including complainants – is second guessing what the likely outcome at the final stage will be. Given this report's finding that trials involving adult victim/witnesses are more likely to result in an acquittal, these concerns are anything but groundless. Whilst the police, and to some extent the CPS, have begun to address ways in which they can improve their response to rape, these efforts will not have a major impact unless the complex interactions between each stage of the process are understood.

An unexpected finding, which deserves more attention than can be given here (see also Finney, 2004), was that alcohol was involved in over one-third of cases reported to the police (34%, n=891). Drugs were suspected in over one in ten (12%, n=312): in a significant proportion of these (36%, n=111), the presence of drugs was either not confirmed by toxicology tests or limited to recreational use, often combined with alcohol.[48]

---

48. Higher rates of involvement of alcohol and drugs were revealed in the St Mary's data, where there was wider access to accurate details in a greater number of cases. Here, alcohol was involved in over half of cases reported to the police where a forensic examination was carried out (56%, n=595), while drugs were suspected in around one-fifth (18%, n=198), with recreational drug use apparent in 40 per cent (n=79) of these.

At minimum alcohol is three times more associated with rape than drugs, and probably closer to four times, but little, if any, work has addressed this correlation. Two aspects that deserve closer examination are the additional correlation of alcohol with rapes by recent acquaintances (55%, n=162), and that the presence of alcohol increased the levels of recorded injuries (51%, n=450). In addition, analysis of statements and data from service users suggest there is a group of predatory men who target women when they are drunk, so drunk in a number of cases that their capacity to consent had to be impaired. There were indications of a range of potential targeting strategies involved, which deserve further study. For example, two of the interviewees were women in their fifties, returning home from a night out with friends. In both instances a man presented himself as trustworthy, and in one case he offered to ensure she got home safely. She was subsequently raped in her own home. Lawyer and author Andrew Vasschs terms this pattern 'targeted predation', and comments:

> Rapists see two different forms of weakness: (1) she's drunk and (2) she's drunk. Meaning, she's physically impaired because of the alcohol, but also no one is going to believe her because they disapprove of her drinking.
>
> (Personal communication, September 2003)

Attrition in context

Attrition is a process within which institutional rules, previous and predicted experience and gendered expectations of behaviour interact. Police, CPS, judges (and presumably juries) all work with 'gender schemes' which set the boundaries of what is considered appropriate and inappropriate behaviour for men and women. Jeffner's (2000) research with young people in Sweden, suggests that the same factors provide men with more of what she terms 'space for action', whilst simultaneously narrowing and restricting the space available for women. In relation to rape these factors include: alcohol; previous consensual sex; reputation; and mental health issues. Where these factors are present – whether for men or women – sex without consent is normalised, as being something other than 'rape'. She concludes that despite young people in Sweden defining rape on a general philosophical level as any sex that happens after a woman has said no, when invited to explore this in relation to specific contexts:

> Only a sober young woman, who does not have a bad reputation, who has not behaved sexually provocatively and who has said no in the right way can be raped, and only by a young man who is sober and 'deviant' and with whom she is not in love. (Jeffner, 2000)

The malleability of rape, and the meaning of consent, were also evident in research with young people in the UK and Ireland (Burton *et al.*, 1998; Regan and Kelly, 2001), illustrating that notions of 'real rape' not only reinforce the normative stereotype referred to earlier, but also designate conditions under which non-consensual sex is 'not really rape'.

It is the awareness of these realities, and the fact that their credibility will be questioned in court (and, potentially, their sexual history raised), that was the most potent reason behind women's decisions to withdraw their complaint. Very early decisions to not complete the initial elements of an investigation are influenced by careless and insensitive treatment by police officers, as well as an existing perception of not being able to face any potential court process. Examples were uncovered of miscommunications, where police officers, in good faith[49], honestly conveyed the unlikelihood of a conviction and the difficulty of the court experience. These messages, whilst accurate, especially when given at a very early point (for example during or after taking an initial complaint or statement), are perceived by the victim as indicating disbelief at worst and as discouragement from engaging in the legal process at best.

There was little evidence of inter-agency links between police and CPS that sought to build cases; to find evidence that might go to the credit and believability of the complainant. Rather, all too often, the focus appeared to be on what was discrediting. There is evidence from other jurisdictions that a focus on building cases, especially when applied to those where consent is the likely defence, can increase the level of prosecutions and convictions.[50]

> *For generations, sexual assault or rape was and continues to be defined in our minds as a violent and unprovoked attack by a stranger on defenceless, vulnerable, and unsuspecting victim. Our understanding of this crime … influences (even without conscious intent) our attempts to investigate and evaluate sexual assaults … We found officers were looking for serious injury, weapons and immediate cries for help to establish the elements of force or fear and to judge the 'believability' of the victim … and missing the opportunity to collect, describe, or emphasize the very necessary evidence that would support the lack of consent* (Archambault and Lindsay, 2001).

In terms of understanding early withdrawal, there is no doubt that there has been a shift in policing to victim care/satisfaction and the impact is palpable in the more positive assessments from our questionnaire respondents, especially with respect to the earliest stages of intervention, compared to studies conducted in the late 1980s and early 1990s.

49. Good faith is presumed here, although previous research in the US has suggested that some police officers use this as a deliberate strategy to encourage withdrawal (Kersetter, 1990).
50. See for example, Archambault and Faugno, 2001; Archambault and Lindsay, 2001 with respect to San Diego.

Far less attention has been given to improving investigation[51], and it is at this point in the process that considerably more dissatisfaction is expressed (see also Jordan, 2001b for similar findings with respect to New Zealand). The lack of knowledge transfer within the domestic violence field, especially with respect to enhanced evidence-gathering and supporting complainants to remain in the system, is also worth noting. This study confirmed that there are two major points of intense disappointment and loss of confidence that contribute to the decision of victims/survivors to withdraw their trust and co-operation: where the early investigative processes explicitly or implicitly suggest that women are not telling the truth and/or that the case is not worth pursuing; and later when a failure to keep them informed, to show that the CJS cares and/or ambivalence in the investigative officers leads to a loss of faith.

Perhaps the greatest challenge to the CJS is to re-think what rape is, and from this to then develop new understandings of how to approach, investigate and prosecute it.

Key findings

- There are false allegations, and possibly slightly more than some researchers and support agencies have suggested. However, at maximum they constitute nine per cent and probably closer to three per cent of all reported cases. An over-estimation of the scale by police officers and prosecutors feeds into a culture of scepticism, which in turn leads to poor communication and loss of confidence between complainants and the police.
- In areas with integrated SARCs fewer complainants declined to complete the initial process, and two SARC areas had slightly higher conviction rates.
- When given at an early point, honest assessments by police officers of the likelihood of conviction and the difficulties of a prosecution are interpreted by complainants as discouragement to continue with the case.
- There was little evidence of attempts to build cases, and some evidence of poor investigation and understanding of the law, with clear emphasis in some cases entirely on what was discrediting.
- Whilst there are many reasons why victims/survivors withdraw their co-operation, fear of the trial process and discouragement by the police featured strongly.
- Police categorisation of cases is internally inconsistent, making monitoring and evaluation extremely problematic.

---

51. Project Sapphire in the Metropolitan police is beginning to move in this direction, but in the first years prioritised ensuring consistent and sensitive responses and developing SARCs.

- Few cases involved women with learning difficulties or women with mental health problems (see also Harris and Grace, 1999).

Intellectual disability and psychiatric instability ... tend to be viewed as diminishing the victim's credibility, rather than enhancing her vulnerability.

(Jordan, 2001b, p349)

- None of the gang rapes with more than three assailants resulted in convictions.
- Women whose cases went to trial expressed disquiet and a strong sense of injustice that they had no contact with the prosecution barrister[52], and the majority of those where the outcome was an acquittal complained of weak prosecution advocacy in the courtroom.
- All stages of the attrition process appear more marked for young women, particularly those aged 16 to 25, who are highly represented in cases involving false allegations, early and late withdrawal of complaints and acquittals. This requires strategies to address the way this age group is responded to and supported through the CJS.
- Alcohol consumption was present in a much larger number of cases than drugs – either voluntarily consumed or administered to facilitate rape. One would not, however, know this from recent media coverage or police awareness-raising campaigns. The ways in which consumption of alcohol contributes to all points of attrition deserves more detailed study.

Good practice is possible

Given that the focus of this study has been attrition, most attention has been on the factors that account for cases being lost or dropped. The evaluation of SARCs (see Lovett *et al.*, 2004) also contains lessons about elements of practice that make a positive difference.

Poor practice erodes confidence, not just that of complainants with the CJS, but also that of agencies with each other and of the general public. It should be axiomatic that a complainant who is treated in a respectful and compassionate manner, by skilled professionals, is not only less likely to withdraw support from the legal process at a later date, but also more likely to feel able to tell what she knows, and include at the outset any issues which could be seen as discrediting. These are gestures of trust, and unless those

---

52. Recent Bar Council guidelines do now allow for barristers to introduce themselves, but this does not appear to have become routine practice.

responding demonstrate that they are trustworthy, they will not be forthcoming. The police are often the first official point of contact and as such set the tone for subsequent processes.

> A negative police response can compound the trauma suffered by a rape victim, making it less likely that she will decide to proceed with legal action and a strong possibility that her experience will deter others from even making the initial police contact in similar circumstances. If for no other reason, it is in the overall interests of law enforcement for the police to act in ways that are consistent with promoting the victim's emotional well-being.
> (Jordan, 2001b, p75)

> The experience of feeling believed was particularly vital ... Feeling believed was of significant assistance both in dealing with the criminal justice system and also in coping with the trauma of the rape itself.
> (Temkin, 1997, p519)

The research data contain many examples of initial police responses being thoughtful and respectful (70% of questionnaire respondents were satisfied with the initial police response), but the investigative process was experienced much more negatively. The following positive example reveals the significance for complainants of being kept informed and of continued contact.

> The police rang me and kept me in touch and said, "We've not heard anything yet, how are you keeping?" and X [female police officer] she rang every fortnight, just to see how I was. I explained my fears to her about actually going to trial and him getting away with it ... I said, "X, I love to hear from you in some ways, because it's nice to know that you're still bothered and you still care."
> (St Mary's, Service User Interview 1, Acquittal)

Compare this with the far greater number of questionnaire respondents and interviewees (n=23) who had the opposite experience of communication from the police.

> My argument is with the police. And the way they've treated me ... If they'd have kept me informed then maybe I wouldn't have been as annoyed with them ... And they probably might have made me feel better if I still thought that they cared.
> (St Mary's, Service User Interview 3, Undetected)

> And then they kind of just disappeared for ages, I mean, about three weeks after that I called X [SOLO officer] and she said she had nothing to do with it anymore but she'd try and get them to ring me. And they didn't. And nobody was telling me

anything, I didn't speak to them for like four weeks before they came to work, and then I don't think I ever spoke to them again after that … That really was it for ages … I was always really scared of phoning, because when I phoned I would sort of say "Can I speak to so-and-so please?" and it would be like "Oh, there's nobody in, and what's it about?" and I wouldn't really know what to say … It just seemed to me to be all wrong, that they were a service provider and I was almost having to, I don't know … I almost felt like I was putting them out, because every time I spoke to them they were telling me how busy they were.

(REACH, Service User Interview 8, Undetected)

I am a bit annoyed because the only way I have found out about the courts is through the STAR helpline. The police have not been in touch, only once has someone come to see me and that was to take another statement for the CPS about how I have been after the attack. I thank STAR for the case tracking – at least I know when the court dates are and what is happening. (STAR, Q1, 2085, Conviction)

I think the police handled my case very badly, at first when they found out about the rape they were very eager for me to press charges. Then after a few weeks they didn't seem at all interested. When the case went to court the DC didn't even turn up for the trial. I was furious the police did not telephone me to tell me the outcome. This was very important to me as I needed to obtain an emergency injunction against my attacker. Because the police failed to contact me this injunction was delayed for two days, which was very upsetting and frightening for me.

(Comparison 3, Q2, 4016, Detected no proceedings)

Some of the participants were insightful about why these problems persist, and how they could be overcome.

The crime of rape is still very much a difficult process to go through, the police are still in the dark ages and you are still very much made to feel that somehow you are to blame, that you could have prevented it. The police really need to look into the training of officers and how as a unit of trust they can improve on this. It's hard enough to admit to being raped without someone doubting you. It's no wonder so many people don't report it … STAR at least listens in a non-judgemental way, and listens to you, never doubting. They are really understanding and helpful and just having someone believe you can help you live again. Without STAR, I would have completely fallen apart. (STAR, Q1, 2065, Status unknown)

The comments about SARCs reveal that it is the tone and content of human interaction, the sense of being respected and treated as someone who is more than 'just a victim' which was not only appreciated, but enabled women to cope with lengthy and difficult demands, such as a forensic examination.

> And the respect I was shown! I didn't respect myself, you see, so for somebody to show you that much respect, and kindness, you start thinking, "I'm not a bad person, I'm not this dirty person, I thought I was, tainted, violated. They're treating me as normal." Something terrible has happened but they're treating me normally! And you get a little bit – you feel confident, and more in control of things.
>
> (St Mary's, Service User Interview 11, Acquittal)

What complainants value and need

The information from questionnaires and interviews about aspects of current service provision that were strongly valued has been summarised here, along with suggestions on how responses to reported rape could be improved.

- Availability of female police officers and forensic examiners.
- A private, calming environment.
- A culture of belief and support.
- Being treated as a whole person, and "as a person not a case".
- Respect – strongly distinguished from being patronised, or condescended to.
- Being 'in control' of the forensic examination.
- Technological innovation to make the statement taking process less protracted, i.e. the police officer not having to write everything down in longhand, and to be in the words of the complainant.
- Access to a simple card or flyer with a phone number where support and information would be easily accessible, including out of hours.
- Awareness of the meaning of information, and the time it is most appropriate to give it, especially where police officers are providing a realistic assessment of the prospects of prosecution and conviction.
- Services keeping proactive contact and being kept informed about case progress (see Lovett et al., 2004).
- Continuity of police officers, and meeting investigative officers in person.
- Being able to re-read statements the week before trial or at least not in the hour before giving evidence.
- Contact with prosecution barristers.

- Prosecution barristers being familiar with the facts of the case and courtroom advocacy that does 'justice' to the complainant's account.
- Building cases, pursuing supporting evidence and presenting a believable narrative that explains the behaviour of the complainant.

Many of these elements constitute what has been termed 'procedural justice', and this research confirms the significance of a sense of procedural fairness to victims' perceptions of the CJS. The summary below, from a study of women's satisfaction with how domestic violence cases were dealt with in Canberra, Australia echoes the perceptions of those in this study who reported rape.

> *Victim/witnesses seek* notification *on a range of things – dates, decision-making points, decisions (charge, prosecution, bail, court outcome), and identities of key participants. Linked to notification is the need for* information *about the system, how it works, the role of the prosecution and of the victim/witness ... In the main, victim/witnesses also seek opportunities for* participation *through making the initial complaint to police, the provision of a full statement, offering (or not) background, consultation on their views and opinions, input at bail, input at post conviction through the Victim Impact Statement and (occasionally) the Pre-Sentence Report ...* Respectful acknowledgement *relates to the inter-personal communication between the victim/witness and justice practitioner. This idea stresses the style of the interaction – for example, the extent to which the communication is empathetic and builds rapport.*
> (Holder and Mayo, 2003, original emphasis, p18)

The fact that these may be more, or at least as, important as eventual outcomes is evidenced by the responses of those women whose cases resulted in acquittals, but who were supported throughout by the Support Worker at St Mary's. Whilst all were disappointed with the outcome, none regretted pursuing the case. This contrasts sharply with research participants whose cases were dropped or lost at an earlier point, and who encountered limited support: many of them were profoundly dissatisfied with the responses they encountered, reporting that if they were ever sexually assaulted again they would not report, and that they would discourage any friend from doing so. The research interviews also highlighted the extent to which women are aware of the low conviction rate. If the attrition rate continues to increase, and if the layers of the criminal justice system fail to address their role in it, erosion of confidence will expand, as will the numbers of those whose designation as having made a 'previous allegation' means any subsequent report is treated with scepticism.

The attrition process is currently reproducing itself and in the process is creating a justice gap that is experienced by many rape complainants as more like a chasm. From the perspective of practitioners and policy-makers, however, the authors explication of the layers involved in attrition suggests that this distance is made up of a series of distinct, whilst connected, gaps. Addressing each of these systematically, rather than attempting to bridge the chasm in one leap, is more likely to produce improvements. The recommendations below are offered as initial steps to reverse the trend of falling conviction rates.

Recommendations

1. The most important recommendation from this study in terms of the investigation of rape complaints is that a shift occurs from an exercise in scepticism focusing on discreditability to enhanced evidence-gathering and case-building. Within this three working groups are suggested to develop guidelines and resources to support this change of emphasis.
   - To rethink the entire process of rape investigation and prosecution through the lens of known offenders and consent defences. This group should include police, CPS, barristers, forensic scientists, academics and the voluntary sector.
   - To develop, drawing on international experience and the disability sector, policy and advice on investigating and prosecuting cases where complainants have learning disabilities and/or mental health problems.
   - The development of new rape examination kits, which can be used flexibly depending on the facts of the case and likely defence. Elements should include agreed national forms for forensic examiners, which should accompany any samples sent to the forensic science service (see Kelly, 2003b for more detailed discussion).

2. The possibility of inter-agency work between police and specialist support agencies should be further explored with respect to providing support during statement-taking and providing information on case status (see also Lovett *et al.*, 2004).

3. Home Office counting rules for rape and sexual offences need to be revisited in light of the findings from this research: whether cases where there is no evidence of assault should remain needs to be addressed, and mechanisms should be developed to correct inconsistent classification.

4. Reflection on, and guidance issued, within the police about the timing and content of providing complainants with information about the legal process and the likelihood of a conviction. At a number of points, from the earliest contact on, this was perceived by victims/witnesses as discouragement from proceeding with the case.

5. Development in all areas, through SARCs and/or Rape Crisis Centres, of proactive follow-up of all complainants reporting rape to the police. Such services would add the most value if they combined practical support, advocacy and case tracking (see also Lovett et al., 2004).

6. Piloting of early case conferences between police, CPS and counsel, to explore potential evidential weaknesses, and whether these might be addressed through additional evidence, expert testimony, research findings or courtroom advocacy.

7. An accredited training course for prosecution barristers, and the development of some form of sanction where briefs are returned or counsel changed just before trial.

8. Mechanisms within CPS to both monitor and evaluate courtroom prosecution advocacy, and to learn lessons from convictions and acquittals, and especially guilty pleas.

9. Increased recognition of the significance of alcohol in rape and sexual assault, including within the government's proposed alcohol policy. This should also include further exploration of the extent to which men target unknown women who are drinking, and the strategies they use to make initial contact.

10. Last, but certainly not least, in light of the Sex Offences Act, development of a public education campaign on the meaning of consent and realities of rape, alongside more detailed training for CJS personnel, explicitly designed to expand the concept of 'real rape'.

Appendices

Appendix 1

Appendix 1: Notifiable Offences and Numbers of Persons Prosecuted, Tried and Convicted for Rape Offences in England and Wales, 2001 and 2002, including reporting and conviction rates

2001	Notifiable Offences	Number Prosecutions (2)	Number Tried (3)	Guilty pleas (4) Number convicted	Plea data not available Number tried	Number convicted	Not guilty pleas (4) Number tried	Number convicted	Total convictions	% Conviction rate	Notifiable offences per 100,000	Population mid-2001
England & Wales	9,449	2,651	1,380	213	11	3	1,156	356	572	6.05	18.14	52,084,900
Avon & Somerset	305	96	34	6	0	0	28	9	15	4.92	20.56	1,483,500
Bedfordshire	94	25	17	3	0	0	14	8	11	11.70	16.60	566,400
Cambridgeshire	141	33	11	3	0	0	8	4	7	4.96	19.86	710,000
Cheshire	74	36	25	4	0	0	21	3	7	9.46	7.52	983,700
Cleveland	41	21	12	0	0	0	12	5	5	12.20	7.57	541,300
Cumbria	49	38	12	1	0	0	11	5	6	12.24	10.05	487,800
Derbyshire	119	38	15	1	1	0	13	3	4	3.36	12.44	956,600
Devon & Cornwall	163	35	34	7	0	0	27	6	13	7.98	10.33	1,578,600
Dorset	93	41	11	3	0	0	8	1	4	4.30	13.41	693,500
Durham	49	38	13	1	0	0	12	2	3	6.12	8.28	591,600
Dyfed Powys	43	16	11	0	1	0	10	2	2	4.65	8.81	488,300
Essex	217	47	21	4	0	0	17	5	9	4.15	13.43	1,616,200
Gloucestershire	52	14	4	1	1	0	2	0	1	1.92	9.20	565,000
Greater Manchester	542	164	84	16	0	0	68	26	42	7.75	21.83	2,482,800
Gwent	98	41	23	1	0	0	22	8	9	9.18	17.74	552,500
Hampshire	305	108	59	6	0	0	53	17	23	7.54	17.15	1,778,200
Hertfordshire	84	28	18	2	0	1	16	5	8	9.52	8.12	1,034,900
Humberside	149	22	19	3	0	0	16	5	8	5.37	17.14	869,100

Kent	181	48	45	3	1	41	16	20	11.05	11.45	1,580,900
Lancashire	211	90	43	6	0	37	14	20	9.48	14.91	1,415,600
Leicestershire	158	50	21	3	1	17	3	6	3.80	17.09	924,700
Lincolnshire	100	21	12	1	0	11	4	5	5.00	15.44	647,600
Merseyside	281	85	56	8	0	48	20	28	9.96	20.64	1,361,700
Metropolitan Police (5)	2,462	447	233	31	2	200	58	89	3.61	34.25	7,188,000
Norfolk	124	24	16	4	0	12	1	5	4.03	15.54	797,900
North Wales	127	27	9	0	0	9	3	3	2.36	19.14	663,500
North Yorkshire	52	26	19	4	0	15	3	7	13.46	6.92	751,400
Northamptonshire	88	6	14	5	0	9	4	9	10.23	13.96	630,400
Northumbria	269	79	52	12	1	39	10	22	8.18	19.44	1,383,700
Nottinghamshire	251	79	47	14	0	33	15	29	11.55	24.71	1,015,800
South Wales	122	87	35	5	0	30	6	11	9.02	10.18	1,198,800
South Yorkshire	125	59	40	5	2	33	12	17	13.60	9.87	1,266,500
Staffordshire	231	63	23	5	0	18	4	9	3.90	22.05	1,047,600
Suffolk	107	25	16	1	0	15	0	1	0.93	15.98	669,400
Surrey	126	26	17	2	0	15	5	7	5.56	11.89	1,059,500
Sussex	245	49	24	3	0	21	6	9	3.67	16.38	1,495,500
Thames Valley	286	62	28	5	0	23	11	16	5.59	13.67	2,092,900
Warwickshire	24	5	2	2	0	0	0	2	8.33	4.74	506,200
West Mercia	156	50	25	6	0	19	2	8	5.13	13.46	1,159,000
West Midlands	616	213	108	15	0	93	29	44	7.14	24.12	2,554,400
West Yorkshire	406	168	63	9	1	53	15	25	6.16	19.52	2,080,200
Wiltshire	83	21	9	2	0	7	3	3	3.61	13.52	613,700

(1) Apart from notifiable offence figures, all other figures are based on the number of cases where a rape offence is the principal offence.
(2) Number prosecuted for rape offences, appearing at the Magistrates Court in 2001.
(3) Offence is recorded at Crown Court outcome, rather than at start of trial. Cases where a trial for a rape offence is reduced to a non-rape offence will not be included here. In addition, the year of trial may be different to that of the prosecution.
(4) Guilty pleas are those recorded at any point; both timeous and late guilty pleas are included.
(5) Includes City of London (8 notifiable offences, 0 prosecutions).

2002	Notifiable Offences	Number Prosecutions (2)	Number Tried (3)	Guilty pleas [4] Number convicted	Plea data not available Number tried	Number convicted	Not guilty pleas [4] Number tried	Number convicted	Total convictions	% Conviction rate	Notifiable offences per 100,000	Population mid-2002
England & Wales	11,766	2,945	1,079	258	3	4	818	393	655	5.57	22.41	52,480,474
Avon & Somerset	396	86	28	6	0	0	22	7	13	3.28	26.57	1,490,367
Bedfordshire	107	31	8	3	0	0	5	4	7	6.54	18.75	570,831
Cambridgeshire	214	24	16	5	1	0	10	4	9	4.21	29.88	716,285
Cheshire	110	35	15	3	0	0	12	7	10	9.09	11.16	986,079
Cleveland	89	35	18	4	0	0	14	7	11	12.36	16.45	541,172
Cumbria	60	27	10	2	0	0	8	4	6	10.00	12.28	488,513
Derbyshire	168	44	18	7	0	0	11	2	9	5.36	17.46	962,502
Devon & Cornwall	277	17	31	5	1	1	25	11	17	6.14	17.41	1,590,699
Dorset	142	30	9	2	0	0	7	6	8	5.63	20.39	696,327
Durham	76	39	11	1	0	0	10	4	5	6.58	12.88	590,201
Dyfed Powys	60	21	6	0	0	0	6	3	3	5.00	12.14	494,122
Essex	250	60	7	4	0	1	3	2	7	2.80	15.41	1,622,403
Gloucestershire	114	32	9	0	0	0	9	2	2	1.75	20.1	566,977
Greater Manchester	667	203	63	15	0	0	48	21	36	5.40	26.54	2,513,468
Gwent	125	53	26	8	0	0	18	8	16	12.80	22.56	554,036
Hampshire	327	112	45	9	0	0	36	19	28	8.56	18.27	1,789,678
Hertfordshire	168	35	15	2	0	0	13	8	10	5.95	16.21	1,036,144
Humberside	249	38	19	4	0	0	15	8	12	4.82	28.6	870,671
Kent	213	77	29	7	0	0	22	13	20	9.39	13.4	1,589,252
Lancashire	234	98	35	10	0	0	25	7	17	7.26	16.46	1,421,912

Leicestershire	244	55	15	4	0	11	5	9	3.69	26.13	933,749
Lincolnshire	137	35	13	2	0	11	8	10	7.30	20.83	657,843
Merseyside	334	103	39	7	0	32	10	17	5.09	24.54	1,361,009
Metropolitan Police (5)	2,690	578	208	42	1	166	76	119	4.42	36.57	7,355,354
Norfolk	167	21	14	4	0	10	6	10	5.99	20.8	802,766
North Wales	124	30	12	4	0	8	3	7	5.65	18.55	668,303
North Yorkshire	116	28	18	3	0	15	7	10	8.62	15.36	755,332
Northamptonshire	171	4	13	5	0	8	3	8	4.68	26.79	638,238
Northumbria	320	64	34	14	0	20	11	25	7.81	23.16	1,381,901
Nottinghamshire	241	63	25	5	0	20	10	15	6.22	23.55	1,023,160
South Wales	179	101	34	11	0	23	11	22	12.29	14.88	1,202,262
South Yorkshire	179	63	30	7	0	23	15	22	12.29	14.13	1,267,288
Staffordshire	240	60	23	4	1	19	9	14	5.83	22.91	1,047,528
Suffolk	138	36	14	4	0	10	3	7	5.07	20.54	671,931
Surrey	126	27	7	3	0	4	3	6	4.76	11.89	1,059,900
Sussex	328	53	13	4	0	9	8	12	3.66	21.87	1,499,997
Thames Valley	355	52	27	6	0	21	12	18	5.07	16.91	2,099,559
Warwickshire	60	10	1	0	0	1	1	1	1.67	11.7	512,680
West Mercia	219	49	20	5	1	15	8	13	5.94	18.75	1,168,148
West Midlands	696	250	61	14	0	46	20	34	4.89	27.02	2,575,768
West Yorkshire	515	134	30	8	0	22	12	20	3.88	24.65	2,089,212
Wiltshire	141	32	10	5	0	5	5	10	7.09	22.86	616,907

(1) Apart from notifiable offence figures, all other figures are based on the number of cases where a rape offence is the principal offence.
(2) Number prosecuted for rape offences, appearing at the Magistrates Court in 2001.
(3) Offence is recorded at Crown Court outcome, rather than at start of trial. Cases where a trial for a rape offence is reduced to a non-rape offence will not be included here. In addition, the year of trial may be different to that of the prosecution.
(4) Guilty pleas are those recorded at any point; both timeous and late guilty pleas are included.
(5) Includes City of London (3 prosecutions).

Appendix 2

Appendix 2: Comparative profile of all six study sites

Profile	Greater Manchester	Northumbria	West Yorkshire	Brent	Newham	Thames Valley[1]
Total population[2]	2,482,328	1,383,128	2,079,211	263,464	243,891	2,091,689
People aged 16-74	1,781,882 (72%)	1,009,986 (73%)	1,489,740 (72%)	198,712 (75%)	170,268 (70%)	1,528,836 (73%)
Ethnic origin						
White	2,260,507 (91%)	1,346,183 (97%)	1,842,813 (89%)	119,278 (45%)	96,130 (39%)	1,914,756 (92%)
Black and other minority ethnic	221,821 (9%)	36,945 (3%)	236,398 (11%)	144,186 (55%)	147,761 (61%)	176,933 (8%)
Geographical area	1,276 sq kilometres	5,553 sq kilometres	2,029 sq kilometres	43 sq kilometres	36 sq kilometres	3,520 sq kilometres
Area type	Metropolitan	Urban and rural	Urban and rural	Metropolitan	Metropolitan	Urban and rural
Reported rapes 2001[3]	542	269	406	105	93	286
Cases in study sample 2001[4]	351	144	339	62	34	57

Notes

1. The area covered by Thames Valley Police spans parts of the three counties of Berkshire, Buckinghamshire and Oxfordshire, but does not correspond exactly with local authority or county areas as used by the UK Census 2001. Data from Aylesbury Vale, Bracknell Forest, Cherwell, Chiltern, Milton Keynes, Oxford, Reading, Windsor & Maidenhead, Slough, South Bucks, South Oxfordshire, Vale of White Horse, West Berkshire, West Oxfordshire, Wokingham and Wycombe have been aggregated here to represent the closest possible replication of the area served by this police force.

2. Source of data on population, age and ethnic origin and geographical area for all sites: http://www.statistics.gov.uk/census2001/.

3. Figures on reported rapes in Greater Manchester, Northumbria, West Yorkshire and Thames Valley from Home Office data, covering calendar year 2001. Figures on reported rapes in Brent and Newham from Metropolitan Police Rape/Sexual Offences Statistics Package covering financial year 2001/2002.

4. This is the number of individuals at each site that are recorded on the authors' case-tracking database who made a report of rape to the police. This has been calculated for the calendar year 2001 for Greater Manchester, Northumbria, West Yorkshire (see above note); for Brent, Newham and Thames Valley the authors' data collection began On 1st September 2001, so the figures presented relate to the period of a year from 1st September 2001 to 31st August 2002.

Appendix 3:   Research tools and data sources

St Mary's historic database

St Mary's has their own database containing details of all cases who have been referred to the Centre since it opened in late 1986. The original database ran on a FoxPro system, which is now obsolete. In 2003 this was replaced with a new Access database, designed by an external consultant, and all original data were imported. The new database contains a similar range of fields to those in the case-tracking database, which are organised around the following four main areas:

- *Attendance and personal details* – SARC number, referral type, attendance date and time, age, sex, ethnic origin, disability, relationship profile, employment status and area of residence.
- *Assault details* – date and time it occurred, type of assault, area it occurred in, type of location, number of assailants, relationship between assailant and victim, and use of weapon and force.
- *Police details* – date of report, crime number, Force Wide Incident number, type of offence recorded, statement details, crime classification, and court and sentencing details.
- *Forensic details* – examination date and time, nature of incident, and details on the presence of alcohol, drugs and injuries.

Case-tracking database

The case-tracking database was created specifically for this project using Access software to include details on all cases being referred to the three SARCs and being reported in the Comparison areas. Every individual entered on the database has a record consisting of a header and a series of linked forms. The header contains: the unique reference number; research site; referral type; and details of participation in the evaluation. The linked forms and fields within them focus on:

- *Details of the assault* – date and time it occurred, location, type and additional details.
- *Details of the victim* – age, sex, ethnic origin, disability, relationship profile and employment status.

- *Details of the perpetrator(s)* – age, sex, ethnic origin, disability, employment status, relationship to the victim, length of acquaintance and whether a weapon was used.
- *Forensic examination* – date and time of, examiner type, whether injuries were sustained, whether drugs/alcohol were involved and which samples were taken.
- *Service use* – type of service accessed at each site.
- *Police report* – date and time reported, who reported, whether a statement was taken, whether a suspect was identified, arrested and held in custody, CPS advice, reasons for cases not proceeding and additional details on case progress.
- *Legal process* – final police classification, whether the case went to court, plea, trial outcome and sentence.

The level and type of data recorded, as well as the recording systems in place, varied at each site. Consequently, different processes for obtaining the information required for the case-tracking database were employed at the six sites. STAR has its own database that contains many fields comparable to those in the case-tracking database. STAR has a case tracker who informs service users of case progress, therefore, providing the service users have reported the assault, the database contains detailed information on case outcomes. Copies of the STAR database were anonymised by removing the names and contact details of the service users and periodically downloaded for the research team. In the three Comparison areas all data were supplied by the police. At St Mary's and REACH, there were varying degrees of reliance on the police for elements of data, such as details of the police report, perpetrator details and legal outcomes. This information was obtained by distributing two pro formas to police officers, one within a month of the initial police report and the second up to a year later. In a number of cases multiple follow-ups were needed, both to recover outstanding pro formas and to obtain complete information on cases that had not been completed at the time of returning the second pro forma. The remaining details on victims, forensic examinations and service use were provided by the SARCs completing client details sheets. The database has been used mainly for quantitative analysis. However, the free text fields containing qualitative data on reasons for cases not proceeding and additional information on case progress have been subjected to content analysis, which has been used as a supplementary data element in the discussion of research findings relating to the series of Attrition points.

Service user questionnaires

All those included on the case-tracking database were potential participants in this element of the research. Three phased questionnaires were distributed to those service users who agreed to take part at the first, fifth and twelfth month after their initial contact with the

SARCs or report to the police in the Comparison areas. The questionnaires were adapted to reflect the processes and available services at each site, whilst retaining a common core to ensure comparability. They were also designed to be applicable to those who had reported to the police and those who had not. The questionnaires were referenced using the unique reference number to enable them to be linked to cases entered on the case-tracking database. The areas covered in each of the questionnaires were:

Questionnaire 1

- *About you* – age, ethnic origin, disability, relationship profile, employment status.
- *After the assault* – did you tell anyone about the assault before reporting to the police and what was their response.
- *Reporting to the police* – did you report to the police, reasons for reporting, how long after assault was the report made, how was the report made, your state of mind when reporting, how would you rate the response of first police officer you spoke to, satisfaction with the police at this stage, any suggestions for improving the initial police response.
- *Crisis worker* (St Mary's only) – how you understood their role, sex of the crisis worker, did this make a difference, how would you rate their response, satisfaction with crisis worker, how much information did they give you about the next stage of the process.
- *Specialist police officer* (REACH, STAR and comparison areas only) – did you see a specialist officer, when did you see one, how you understood their role, sex of the officer, did this make a difference, how would you rate their response, satisfaction with specialist officer, any suggestions for improving the response of specialist officers.
- *Forensic medical examination* – did you have one, did you have to wait to see an examiner, feelings before the examination, sex of the examiner, did this make a difference, was the process of the examination explained, how you experienced the examination, how would you rate the response of the examiner, satisfaction with examiner, any suggestions for improving examinations.
- *After the forensic medical examination* – contact with specialist officer/crisis worker after the examination, how would you rate their response.
- *Making a statement to the police* – did you make a statement, when did you make one, where did you make one, were you given a choice about the timing and location of the statement taking, feelings before making a statement, sex of the officers present, did this make a difference, how you experienced making a statement, how would you rate the response of the officers taking the statement,

were you given information about the next stage of the process, have you had any contact with the police since the statement, any suggestions for improving the statement-taking process.

- *Use of services* (SARCs only) – which services have you used so far, how would you rate the response of the service provider, any suggestions for improving the service, were there any services you needed that were not provided.
- *Your decisions and the future* – are you intending to pursue the criminal case, if not, why, how are you coping at the moment, what are you finding difficult.
- *About the questionnaire* – are there any additional questions we should have included, how have you found completing the questionnaire, any additional comments.

Questionnaire 2

- *About you* – how are you coping at the moment, what are you finding difficult, are there any areas where you need support.
- *Take-up of services* – have you been in contact with the SARC since completing initial questionnaire, if yes, has this been helpful, which services have you accessed, how would you rate the response of the service provider, were you referred to any other services by the SARC/police, how would you rate their response, have you received any support from family or friends, who has provided the best support so far.
- *Contact with police* – have the police been in contact since completing the initial questionnaire, what about, how would you rate their response, how well have you been kept informed about their case, is there anything more the police could have done.
- *Criminal case* – do you know the current status of the case, if yes, what is it, what are your views on the outcome.
- *About the questionnaire* – are there any additional questions we should have included, how have you found completing the questionnaire, any additional comments.

Questionnaire 3

- *About you* – how are you coping at the moment, what have you found most difficult over the past year, are there any areas where you need support.
- *Take-up of services* – have you been in contact with the SARC since completing the second questionnaire, has this been helpful, have you been in contact with any other services since completing the second questionnaire, what was their response, how would you describe your overall experience of support services over the past year, could anything have been done differently to support you more.

- *Contact with police* – have the police been in contact since completing the second questionnaire, what about, how would you rate their overall response since you reported the assault, could the police have done anything differently to support you more.
- *Criminal case* – has your case been heard in court, if no, what is the current status, if yes, what was the outcome, did you meet the prosecution barrister, did you give evidence, what was your experience of giving evidence, what are your views on the outcome, how would you describe the overall experience of going to court, is there anything that might have made the experience of going to court easier.
- *About the questionnaire* – are there any additional questions we should have included, what has it been like taking part in this research, any additional comments.

Service user interviews

All service users participating in the questionnaire element of the research were also invited to take part in an interview, either face-to-face or over the telephone. This was to gain more detailed qualitative information on their experiences of service use and the criminal justice process. For face-to-face interviews participants were given a choice of locations, including the SARC, their own home or counselling premises. A letter explaining what taking part in the interview would involve and a return form were distributed with the second of the three service user questionnaires. The interviews were semi-structured and slightly adapted in order to be relevant to service users at the different sites. Interview transcripts were anonymised and referenced using the unique reference number, so they could be linked to completed questionnaires and the case-tracking database. All interviews covered the following broad themes.

- Decision-making about reporting to the police.
- Experience of initial contact with the police.
- Experience of contact with the SARC.
- Response of crisis worker/specialist police officer.
- Experience of giving a statement to the police.
- Follow-up contact/support from the SARC, police and elsewhere.
- Decision-making about the legal process.
- Current status of the case.
- How they are feeling/coping.
- Comments on the process so far.
- What victims of rape/sexual assault need. How did their experience compare with this.
- How the process could be improved.

Witness statements

A sample of witness statements made by victims to the police in the SARC areas was obtained. It was not possible to acquire a random sample of statements for two reasons. Firstly, to avoid disclosure that might affect any proceeding case, the research team was only allowed access to statements in completed cases. In addition, SARC managers requested that consent was obtained from service users to access this material, which limited cases to where the victim/survivor had opted into the evaluation and/or gave permission for the statement to be disclosed. All statements received were anonymised, with the complainant's name removed and were coded with the unique identifier so they could be linked to the other data sources.

Forensic medical reports

Different protocols were negotiated at each SARC site for accessing forensic medical reports, largely reflecting the varying systems for conducting examinations. At St Mary's, copies of all forensic medical reports are stored centrally. Here, all cases where a forensic examination was conducted during the evaluation period were grouped according to examiner type (female doctor or forensic nurse) and then according to final police classification ('no crime', undetected, 'detected no proceedings' and detected). Random sampling was then conducted within these groups and a roughly equal number of reports selected from each. At REACH and STAR, consent to access these documents was sought from service users directly in the same way as for the witness statements (see above), therefore the sample size was more limited. Reports relating to participating service users at REACH were sought from the individual forensic examiners, as they retain all documentation relating to the examinations they have conducted. In the STAR area, where the SARC does not control the conduct of forensic examinations, lengthy negotiations were held with Heathcall, the contractor used to supply forensic examinations in West Yorkshire, regarding access to forensic medical reports. Unfortunately, no reports were forthcoming by the end of the evaluation from this area. All forensic medical reports received were anonymised, removing both the service user and forensic examiner's names, and referenced with the unique identifier to enable cross-referencing with the case-tracking database and other data sources.

Interviews with service providers

Phased semi-structured interviews were conducted with SARC staff (management, counsellors, crisis workers, case tracker and support worker and forensic medical examiners) and key players (police officers, Crown Prosecutors and Victim Support). At St Mary's interviews were conducted at three stages during the evaluation – at the beginning, at a mid-point and at the end. In the REACH and STAR areas interviews were conducted at a mid-point and at the end of the evaluation. In the Comparison areas senior officers were interviewed at a mid-point and at the end of the evaluation, whilst investigative officers and police chaperones/specialist officers were interviewed once.

For SARC staff the interview questions covered the following themes.

- Role in and length of involvement with SARC.
- Contribution of SARCs.
- Any noticeable changes while they have been in post in the type of rape/sexual assault cases they see.
- System for providing forensic examinations.
- Reasons why rape/sexual assault is under-reported.
- Reasons why complaints are withdrawn.
- Reasons why cases are lost later in the criminal justice process.
- Progress and impact of CRP-funded interventions.
- Inter-agency links.

The views of police and other key informants were sought on the following areas.

- Outline of their role.
- Connection with SARC.
- Contribution of SARC and services provided.
- Service offered by police to rape/sexual assault victims in area.
- System for providing forensic examinations.
- Reasons why rape/sexual assault is under-reported.
- Reasons why complaints are withdrawn.
- Reasons why cases are lost later in the criminal justice process.
- Progress and impact of CRP-funded interventions.
- Inter-agency links.

Appendix 4

Appendix 4: Response rates to initial service user questionnaire

	St Mary's		REACH		STAR		Comparison	
	n	%	n	%	n	%	n	%
Total referrals/cases	1,442	100%	638	100%	1,092	100%	355	100%
Invited to participate in evaluation[1]	716	50%	483	76%	829	76%	n/a	n/a
Consented to receive questionnaire pack[2]	343	24%	69	11%	142	13%	37	10%
Returned completed Questionnaire[1]	66	5%	51	8%	91	8%	20	6%
Response rate as proportion of those invited[3]		9%		11%		8%		
Response rate as proportion of those who consented to receive questionnaire pack		19%		74%		64%		54%

Notes

1 At STAR under-16s (STAR 11% of all referrals, n=125) were excluded from the evaluation, as they were the subjects of a separate evaluation of a CRP-funded service for young people. At St Mary's under-16s formed a notable proportion of all service users (St Mary's 18% of all referrals, n=266) and were also not invited to take part due to ethical issues and the question of parental consent. Self-referrals were also excluded until late in the evaluation (22% of total referrals, n=313). These two factors accounted for the difference in the lower numbers of St Mary's service users invited to participate in the evaluation. An additional number of service users at all the SARC sites were not invited either due to other reasons of vulnerability (mental health, learning disability, lack of safe contact address, language) or because the staff member omitted to ask them (St Mary's 8% of all referrals, n=122; REACH 24% of all referrals, n=155; STAR 13% of all referrals, n=138). Unfortunately, police officers in the Comparison areas did not record details of whether or not individual complainants were informed about the evaluation. It is, therefore, impossible to calculate the proportion invited to take part.

2 The difference in the proportions of service users who consented to receive the questionnaire pack is probably reflective of the different protocols for engaging potential participants employed at the three SARCs and in the Comparison areas. At St Mary's consent was sought verbally via the Crisis Worker during first attendance, whereas service users at REACH and STAR and complainants in the Comparison areas were sent written information by the SARCs or police and asked to complete and return a form if they wished to take part. It is possible that being asked to consent to receive the questionnaire pack at the same time as being provided with information on services and options elicited a higher number of positive responses at St Mary's, although these did not translate into an equally high number of completed returns. The REACH and STAR protocol, which gave potential respondents time to consider their involvement, appeared to bring about less agreement to receive the questionnaire pack, although it increased the proportion of completed returns. This difference is particularly marked when the number of completed returns is calculated as a proportion of those who consented to receive the questionnaire pack.

3 Not possible to calculate for Comparison areas.

Appendix 5:

Attrition process – case outcomes for all reported cases

Table 1:   *St Mary's*

n=1,071	N	%	Overall %
Police	**843**		**79%**
No crime	233	100%	22%
False allegation	82	35	
No evidence of assault	54	23	
Insufficient evidence	36	15	
Victim withdrawal	35	15	
Victim declined to complete initial process	20	9	
Other	3	1	
Reason unknown	3	1	
Undetected	294	100%	27%
Victim withdrawal	74	25	
Offender not identified	72	24	
Insufficient evidence	59	20	
Victim declined to complete initial process	39	13	
False allegation	9	3	
No prospect conviction	8	3	
No evidence of assault	3	1	
Reason unknown	30	10	
Detected no proceedings	125	100%	12%
Victim withdrawal	64	51	
Insufficient evidence	22	18	
Victim declined to complete initial process	22	18	
False allegation	3	2	
No prospect conviction	3	2	
Other	1	1	
Reason unknown	10	8	
Detected	21	100%	2%
Victim withdrawal	3	14	
Insufficient evidence	3	14	

Victim declined to complete initial process	2	10	
Not in public interest	1	5	
Other	6	29	
Reason unknown	6	29	
Classification unknown	170	100%	16%
Victim withdrawal	4	2	
Victim declined to complete initial process	3	2	
No prospect conviction	1	1	
Reason unknown	162	95	
CPS	**83**	**100%**	**7%**
Decision unknown	31	37	
Caution/final reprimand	2	2	
Discontinued	8	10	
Victim withdrawal	13	16	
Pending trial	29	35	
Trial	**145**	**100%**	**14%**
Trial to be rearranged, suspect fled	1	1	
Victim withdrawal	10	7	
Discontinued/withdrawn at court	8	5	
Acquittal	49	34	
Guilty plea	46	32	
Not clear if guilty plea/conviction	9	6	
Part conviction	5	3	
Conviction	17	12	
Total convictions	**77**		**7%**

Table 2: REACH

n=380	N	%	Overall %
Police	**321**		**84%**
No crime	82	100%	22%
False allegation	46	56	
No evidence of assault	14	17	
Insufficient evidence	8	10	
Victim withdrawal	7	9	
Victim declined to complete initial process	5	6	
Not in public interest	1	1	
Reason unknown	1	1	
Undetected	90	100%	24%
Insufficient evidence	35	39	
Offender not identified	22	24	
Victim withdrawal	10	11	
Victim declined to complete initial process	9	10	
False allegation	6	7	
No prospect conviction	3	3	
No evidence of assault	1	1	
Reason unknown	4	4	
Detected no proceedings	22	100%	6%
Insufficient evidence	9	41	
Victim withdrawal	7	32	
False allegation	2	9	
Victim declined to complete initial process	2	9	
Not in public interest	1	5	
Reason unknown	1	5	
Detected	13	100%	3%
Insufficient evidence	4	31	
Victim withdrawal	4	31	
Not in public interest	2	15	
Reason unknown	3	23	
Classification unknown	114	100%	30%
False allegation	3	3	
Victim withdrawal	2	2	
Insufficient evidence	2	2	
No evidence of assault	1	1	

No prospect conviction	1	1	
Victim declined to complete initial process	1	1	
Other	1	1	
Reason unknown	103	90	
CPS	**18**	**100%**	**5%**
Decision unknown	3	17	
Discontinued	5	28	
Victim withdrawal	3	17	
Pending trial	7	39	
Trial	**41**	**100%**	**11%**
Discontinued/withdrawn at court	3	7	
Acquittal	18	44	
Guilty plea	12	29	
Part conviction	3	7	
Conviction	5	12	
Total convictions	**20**		**5%**

Table 3:   *STAR*

n=837	N	%	Overall %
Police	**653**		**78%**
No crime	207	100%	25%
Victim declined to complete initial process	66	32	
False allegation	29	14	
Insufficient evidence	17	8	
Victim withdrawal	10	5	
Not in public interest	3	1	
Offender not identified	3	1	
No evidence of assault	2	1	
No prospect conviction	1	0	
Other	44	21	
Reason unknown	32	16	
Undetected	324	100%	39%
Insufficient evidence	112	35	
Offender not identified	89	27	
Victim declined to complete initial process	53	16	
Victim withdrawal	12	4	
False allegation	9	3	
No prospect conviction	9	3	
Not in public interest	5	2	
Other	2	1	
Reason unknown	33	10	
Detected	90	100%	11%
Insufficient evidence	40	44	
Victim withdrawal	20	22	
Victim declined to complete initial process	13	14	
No prospect conviction	7	8	
Not in public interest	5	6	
False allegation	1	1	
Other	3	3	
Reason unknown	1	1	
Classification unknown	32	100%	4%
Insufficient evidence	6	19	
Victim declined to complete initial process	6	19	
Not in public interest	2	6	

Victim withdrawal	2	6	
False allegation	1	3	
No evidence of assault	1	3	
No prospect conviction	1	3	
Offender not identified	1	3	
Other	1	3	
Reason unknown	11	34	
CPS	**57**	**100%**	**7%**
Suspect fled prior to PDH	1	2	
Caution/final reprimand	5	9	
Discontinued	25	44	
Victim withdrawal	7	12	
Pending trial	19	33	
Trial	**127**	**100%**	**15%**
Victim withdrawal	5	4	
Discontinued/withdrawn at court	8	6	
Acquittal	36	28	
Guilty plea	29	23	
Not clear if guilty plea/conviction	8	6	
Part conviction	3	2	
Conviction	38	30	
Total convictions	**78**		**9%**

Table 4: *Amalgamated Comparison area*

n=355	N	%	Overall %
Police	**299**		**84%**
No crime	53	100%	15%
False allegation	18	34	
Victim declined to complete initial process	12	23	
Insufficient evidence	6	11	
No evidence of assault	6	11	
Victim withdrawal	6	11	
Other	2	4	
Reason unknown	3	6	
Undetected	174	100%	49%
Offender not identified	51	29	
Victim declined to complete initial process	42	24	
Victim withdrawal	40	23	
Insufficient evidence	23	13	
False allegation	5	3	
No prospect conviction	3	2	
No evidence of assault	1	1	
Other	2	1	
Reason unknown	7	4	
Detected no proceedings	41	100%	12%
Victim declined to complete initial process	20	49	
Victim withdrawal	13	32	
Insufficient evidence	3	7	
False allegation	2	5	
Other	1	2	
Reason unknown	2	5	
Detected	8	100%	2%
Victim withdrawal	5	8	
Insufficient evidence	1	2	
Offender not identified	1	2	
Other	1	2	
Classification unknown	23	100%	6%
Reason unknown	23	100	

CPS	**47**	**100%**	**13%**
Decision unknown	26	55	
Caution/final reprimand	2	4	
Discontinued	0	0	
Victim withdrawal	2	4	
Pending trial	17	36	
Trial	**9**	**100%**	**3%**
Acquittal	1	11	
Guilty plea	2	22	
Conviction	6	67	
Total convictions	**8**		**2%**

Bibliography

American Medical Association (1995) *Sexual Assault in America.* AMA.

Archambault, J. and Lindsay, S. (2001) 'Responding to non-stranger sexual assault'. In M. Reuland, C. Sole Brito and L. Carroll (eds.), *Solving Crime and Disorder Problems Current Issues, Police Strategies and Organizational Tactics.* PERF. [Available online at: http://www.mysati.com/resources.htm].

Bachman, R. and Paternoster, R. (1993) A Contemporary Look at the Effects of Rape Law Reform: How Far Have We Really Come? *Journal of Criminal Law and Criminology,* 84: 554-574.

Bachman, R. and Smith, P. (1994) The Adjudication of Rape Since Reforms: Examining the Probability of Conviction and Incarceration at the National and Three State Levels. *Criminal Justice Policy Review,* 6: 342-358.

Bergen, R. (1995) 'Surviving wife rape: How women define and cope with the violence'. *Violence Against Women,* 1(2) : 117-138.

Brereton, D. (1993) 'Rape prosecutions in Victoria'. In P. Easteal (ed.) *Without Consent: Confronting Adult Sexual Violence.* Canberra: Australian Institute of Criminology.

Burton, S., Kitzinger, J., Kelly, L. and Regan, L. (1998) *Young People's Attitudes towards Violence, Sex and Relationships: A Survey and Focus Group Study.* Edinburgh: Zero Tolerance Trust.

Burton, S., Regan, L. and Kelly, L. (1998) *Supporting Women and Challenging Men: Lessons from the Domestic Violence Intervention Project.* Bristol:Policy Press.

Caringella-MacDonald, S. (1985) 'Sexual assault prosecution: An examination of model rape legislation in Michigan'. In C. Schweber and C. Feinman (eds.), *Criminal Justice Politics and Women: The Aftermath of Legally Mandated Change* (pp 65-82). New York: Haworth Press.

Chambers, G. and Millar A. (1983) *Investigating Rape.* Edinburgh: HMSO.

Commission on Women and the Criminal Justice System (2004) *Women and the Criminal Justice System.* London: Fawcett Society.

Crown Prosecution Service (2000) *The Code for Crown Prosecutors*. London: CPS.

Department of Women (1996) *Heroines of Fortitude: the Experiences of Women in Court as Victims of Sexual Assault*. Sydney: New South Wales Department of Women.

Du Mont, J. and Myhr, T. (2000) 'So few convictions: The role of client-related characteristics in the legal processing of sexual assaults'. *Violence Against Women*, 6(10): 1109-1136.

Durston, G. (1998) 'Cross-examination of rape complainants: ongoing tensions between conflicting priorities in the criminal justice system'. *Journal of Criminal Law*, 62(1): 91-104.

Esteal, P. (1998) 'Rape in marriage: has the licence lapsed?' In P. Easteal (ed.), *Balancing the Scales: Rape, Law Reform and Australian Culture*. Sydney: Federation Press.

Estrich, S. (1987) *Real Rape: How the Legal System Victimizes Women Who Say No*. Boston: Harvard University Press.

Estrich, S. (1995) 'Is it rape?' In P. Searles and R. Berger (eds.), *Rape and Society: Readings on the Problem of Sexual Assault* (pp 183-193). Boston: Westview Press.

Finney, A. (2004) *Alcohol and Sexual Violence: Key Findings from the Research*. Home Office Findings 215. London: Home Office.

Fisher, B., Cullen, F. and Turner, M. (2000) *The Sexual Victimization of College Women*. Washington DC: Department of Justice.

Frazier, P. and Haney, B. (1996) 'Sexual assault cases in the legal system: police, prosecutor and victim perspectives'. *Law and Human Behaviour*, 20: 607-628.

Frazier, P. and Seales, L. (1997) 'Acquaintance rape is real rape'. In M. Schwartz (ed.), *Researching Sexual Violence Against Women* (pp 54-65). Newbury Park: Sage.

Frohmann, L. (1991) 'Discrediting victims' allegations of sexual assault: prosecutorial accounts of case rejections'. *Social Problems*, 38(2): 213-226.

Grace, S., Lloyd, C. and Smith, L. (1992) *Rape: From Recording to Conviction*. Home Office Research & Planning Unit Paper No 71. London: Home Office.

Greenfield, L. (1997) *Sex Offences and Offenders: An Analysis of Date Rape and Sexual Assault.* US Department of Justice Bureau of Justice Statistics, NCJ-163392.

Gregory, J. and Lees, S. (1999) *Policing Sexual Assault.* London: Routledge.

Hagemann-White, C. (2001) 'European research into the prevalence of violence against women'. *Violence Against Women, 7*(7): 732-759.

Harris, J. and Grace, S. (1999) *A Question of Evidence?: Investigating and Prosecuting Rape in the 1990s.* Home Office Research Study 196. London: Home Office.

HM Crown Prosecution Service Inspectorate and HM Inspectorate of Constabulary (2002) *A Report on the Joint Inspection into the Investigation and Prosecution of Cases involving Allegations of Rape.* London: HMCPSI.

Holder, R. and Mayo, N. (2003) What Do Women Want? Prosecuting Family Violence in the ACT. *Current Issues in Criminal Justice.* 15(1): 5-25.

Home Office (2003) *Home Office Counting Rules for Recorded Crime.* London: Home Office.

Home Office (2002a) *Narrowing the Justice Gap – Framework Document.* London: Home Office.

Home Office (2002b) *Action Plan to implement the recommendations of the HMCPSI/HMIC joint investigation into the investigation and prosecution of cases involving allegations of rape.* London: Home Office

Home Office (1983) *Investigation of the Offences of Rape.* Home Office Circular 25/1983.London: HMSO.

Horney, J. and Spohn, C. (1991) 'Rape law reform and instrumental change in six urban jurisdictions'. *Law and Society Review,* 25(1): 117-153.

Jamieson, L., Burman M., Grundy, S. and Dyer, F. (1998, unpublished) *The 'Attrition' of Sexual Offences in the Criminal Justice System: A Report of a Pilot Study Monitoring Cases from First Report to the Police Final Outcome.* Report submitted to the Scottish Office.

Jeffner, S. (2000) *'Different space for action: The everyday meaning of young people's perception of rape'.* Paper at ESS Faculty Seminar, University of North London, May.

Jewkes, R. and Abrahams, N. (2000) *Violence Against Women in South Africa: Rape and Sexual Coercion – A Review Study.* Crime Prevention Research Resources Centre.

Johnson, H. and Sacco, V. (1995) 'Researching violence against women: Statistics Canada's national study'. *Canadian Journal of Criminology: Special Issue: Focus on the Violence Against Women Survey,* 37(3): 281-304.

Jones, A. (1980) *Women who Kill.* New York: Fawcett, Columbine.

Jordan, J. (1998) *Reporting Rape: Women's Experiences with the Police, Doctors and Support Agencies.* Wellington: Institute of Criminology, Victoria University.

Jordan, J. (2001a) 'Worlds Apart? Women, rape and the police reporting process'. *British Journal of Criminology,* 41: 679-706.

Jordan, J. (2001b) *True 'Lies' and False 'Truths': Women, Rape and the Police.* PhD thesis, Victoria University of Wellington, New Zealand.

Jordan, J. (2002) 'Will any woman do?: Police, gender and rape victims'. *Policing: An International Journal of Police Strategies & Management,* 25(2), 319-344.

Jordan, J. (2004) *The Word of a Woman? Police, Rape and Belief.* London: Palgrave Macmillan.

Katz, S. and Mazur, M. (1979) *Understanding the Rape Victim: Synthesis of Research Findings.* New York: John Wiley.

Kelly, L. (2000) *'Ending the silence, challenging the tolerance: developing community responses in the prevention of domestic violence'.* Keynote paper at International Conference on Violence in the Family: Plan of Action for the 21st Century, Nicosia, Cyprus, November.

Kelly, L. (2002) *A Research Review on the Reporting, Investigation and Prosecution of Rape Cases.* London: HMCPSI.

Kelly, L. (2003a) *Specialisation, Integration and Innovation: Review of Health Service Models for the Provision of Care to Persons who have Suffered Sexual Violence.* Final Report to World Health Organisation.

Kelly, L. (2003b) *Good Practice in Medical Responses to Recently Reported Rape, Especially Forensic Examinations.* Briefing paper for the Daphne Strengthening the Linkages Project conference, Dublin, October.

Kelly, K., Moon G., Bradshaw, Y. and Savage, S. (1998) 'Insult to injury? The medical investigation of rape in England and Wales'. *Journal of Social Welfare and Family Law,* 20(4): 409-20.

Kelly, L. and Regan, L. (2001) *Rape: The Forgotten Issue? A European Attrition and Networking Study.* London: Child and Woman Abuse Studies Unit.

Kersetter, W. (1990) 'Gateway to justice: police and prosecutorial response to sexual assaults against women'. *Journal of Criminal Law and Criminology,* 81: 267-313.

Konradi, A. (1996) 'Preparing to testify: rape survivors negotiating the criminal justice process'. *Gender and Society,* 10(4): 404-432.

Koss, M. (2000) *'Acquaintance rape: a critical update on recent findings with application to advocacy'.* [Available online at: http://www.vip.msu.edu/theCAT/CATAuthor/MPK/colorado.html].

Lea, S., Lanvers, U. and Shaw, S. (2003) 'Attrition in rape cases: developing a profile and identifying relevant factors'. *British Journal of Criminology,* 43: 583-599.

Lees, S. (2002) *Carnal Knowledge: Rape on Trial.* (2nd edition). London: Women's Press.

Lees, S. and Gregory J. (1993) *Rape and Sexual Assault: A Study of Attrition.* London: Islington Council Police and Crime Prevention Unit.

Lovett, J., Regan, L. and Kelly, L. (2004) *Sexual Assault Referral Centres: Developing Good Practice and Maximising Potentials.* Home Office Research Study 285. London: Home Office.

Martin, P. and Powell, R. (1994) 'Accounting for the 'second assault': Legal organizations' framing of rape victims'. *Law and Social Inquiry,* 19: 853-890.

McGregor, M., Du Mont, J. and Myhr, T. (2002) 'Sexual assault forensic medical examination: is evidence related to successful prosecution?' *Annals of Emergency Medicine,* 39(6): 639-647.

Metropolitan Police Service (2002) *MPS Project Sapphire Strategy Action Plan 2002-2003.* London: Metropolitan Police.

Matoesian, G. (1993) *Reproducing Rape: Domination through Talk in the Courtroom.* Chicago: University of Chicago Press.

Myhill, A. and Allen, J. (2002) *Rape and Sexual Assault of Women: the Extent and Nature of the Problem – Findings from the British Crime Survey.* Home Office Research Study 237. London: Home Office.

Painter, K. (1991) *Wife Rape, Marriage and Law: Survey Report, Key Findings and Recommendations.* Manchester University, Department of Social Policy and Social Work.

Regan, L., Lovett, J. and Kelly, L. (2004) *Forensic Nursing: An option for improving responses to reported rape and sexual assault.* Home Office Online Research Report 28/04. [Available online at: http://www.homeoffice.gov.uk/rds/onlinepubs1.html]

Regan, L. and Kelly, L. (2003) *Rape: Still a Forgotten Issue.* Briefing Paper for the Daphne Strengthening the Linkages Project. [Available online at: http://www.rcne.com].

Regan, L. and Kelly, L. (2001) *Teenage Tolerance: The Hidden Lives of Irish Young People.* Dublin: Dublin Women's Aid.

Russell, D. (1984) *Sexual Exploitation.* Beverley Hills, CA: Sage.

Schulhofer, S. (1998) *Unwanted Sex: The Culture of Intimidation and the Failure of Law.* Boston: Harvard University Press.

Schwartz, M. (1997) *Researching Sexual Violence Against Women.* Newbury Park: Sage.

Senate Judiciary Committee (1993) *The Response to Rape: Detours on the Road to Equal Justice.* New York: US Senate. [Available online at: http://www.mith2.umd.edu/WomensStudies/GenderIssues/Violence+Women/ResponsetoRape/full-text].

Simmons, J. and Dodd, T. (2003), *Crime in England and Wales 2002/2003.* Home Office Statistical Bulletin 07/03. London: Home Office.

Sinclair, H. and Bourne, L. (1998) Cycle of Blame or Just World: Effects of Legal Verdicts on Gender Patterns in Rape-Myth Acceptance. *Psychology of Women Quarterly,* 22: 575-588.

Skinner, T. and Taylor, H. (2005) *Providing counselling, support and information to survivors of rape: an evaluation of the Surviving Rape and Trauma After Rape (STAR) Young Person's project.* Home Office Online Research Report. 51/04. [Available online at: http://www.homeoffice.gov.uk/rds/onlinepubs1.html].

Smith, L. (1989) *Concerns about Rape.* Home Office Research Study 106. London: HMSO.

Spohn, C. and Horney, J. (1996) 'The impact of rape law reform on the processing of simple and aggravated rape cases. *Journal of Criminal Law and Criminology,* 86(3): 861-884.

Taslitz, A. (1999) *Rape and the Culture of the Courtroom.* New York: New York University Press.

Temkin, J. (2003) 'Sexual history evidence – beware the backlash'. *Criminal Law Review,* April, 217-242.

Temkin, J. (2002) *Rape and the Legal Process.* Oxford: Oxford University Press.

Temkin, J. (2000a) 'Rape and other sexual assaults: a literature review'. In Home Office, *Setting the Boundaries,* Volume 2. London: HMSO.

Temkin, J. (2000b) 'Prosecuting and defending rape: perspectives from the bar'. *Journal of Law and Society,* 27(2): 219-248.

Temkin, J. (1999) 'Reporting rape in London: a qualitative study'. *Howard Journal of Criminal Justice,* 38(1) 17-41.

Temkin, J. (1998) 'Medical evidence in rape cases: a continuing problem for criminal justice'. *Modern Law Review,* 61: 821-848.

Temkin, J. (1997) 'Plus ca change?: reporting rape in the 1990s'. *British Journal of Criminology,* 37: 507-528.

Tjaden, P. and Thoennes, N. (1998) 'Prevalence, incidence and consequences of violence against women: findings from the national Violence Against Women Survey'. *National Institute of Justice Centers for Disease Control and Prevention: Research in Brief,* pp 1-16.

Ullman, S., Karabatsos, G. and Koss, M. (1999) 'Alcohol and sexual aggression in a national sample of college men'. *Psychology of Women Quarterly,* 23: 673-689.

Vasschs, A. (1994) *Sex Crimes.* New York: Arrow Books.

Walby, S. and Allen, J. (2004) *Domestic violence, sexual assault and stalking: Findings from the British Crime Survey.* Home Office Research Study 276. London: Home Office.

Victim Support (1996) *Women, Rape and the Criminal Justice System.* London: Victim Support.

Women's Unit (1999) *Living Without Fear: An Integrated Approach for Tackling Violence Against Women.* London: Cabinet Office.